Rachel Barnett

Rachel is an English playwright whose plays have been performed in the UK and internationally, including in London at the Hampstead Theatre, the Royal Court, the Arcola Theatre and Polka Theatre. Also at Chichester Festival Theatre, the Hazlitt Theatre in Maidstone, Manhattan Theatre Source in New York, Live Girls in Seattle, and Auroville in India.

She has a wide range of interests which inform her writing. Projects to date have included original work, adaptations, translations, theatre for young audiences and dramaturgy of collaborative devised work.

A sought-after workshop leader, Rachel shares her time between writing, producing, teaching and arts project management.

www.rachelbarnett.co.uk

First published in the UK in 2015 by Aurora Metro Publications Ltd

67 Grove Avenue, Twickenham, TW1 4HX

www.aurorametro.com info@aurorametro.com

Production: Simon Smith, Grace Thiele

With thanks to: Neil Gregory, Hannah Henderson, Maria Borca, Tracey Mulford, Lucia Tunstall.

Rachel Barnett would like to thank: Andrew Barnett-Jones, Judy and Philip Barnett, Dale Rooks, Rupert Rowbotham, Anne Fenton, James Turnbull, Aimee Fairhurst, Andy Pullen and all the young people who have inspired these plays.

10 9 8 7 6 5 4 3 2 1

Printed by 4Edge Limited, Essex, UK

print book ISBN: 978-1-906582-95-1

ebook ISBN: 978-1-906582-79-1

FOUR SHORT PLAYS FOR YOUNG PEOPLE

by

RACHEL BARNETT

AURORA METRO BOOKS

For Toby

CONTENTS

INTRODUCTION

'You can't use up creativity ... the more you use, the more you have.'

Maya Angelou

Rachel Barnett is passionately committed to working with young people and inspiring them with contemporary and vibrant plays. Her writing is brave, bold, poignant and compelling. A strong feature of her work is her superb attention to detail, vivid imagination and wit. Her writing allows directors and young people to capture the world of a play with a uniqueness and originality that makes it refreshing, captivating and engaging for young people. This originates from an exceptional grasp of narrative, deep knowledge and understanding of the dynamics of a scene combined with Rachel's profound interest in human psychology and what compels human behaviour. Additionally, Rachel's enthusiasm and love of literature is inspirational and infectious.

If we accept that children and young people are the audiences, artists and creative workforces of the future, then we, as theatre educators, have a responsibility to introduce and inspire them with meaningful theatre-making experiences and this anthology of new short plays by Rachel Barnett offers exciting possibilities for young people to perform.

Scope for young performers

Inclusive youth theatre activities can provide an essential platform for children and young people to develop a life-long enjoyment and appreciation of the arts. If we are able to develop and nurture a nation of excellent actors, directors, producers, writers, designers, stage managers and technicians, then theatre will remain vibrant and stay alive.

Obviously, there are benefits to those youth theatre activities which take place in a working theatre that provides access to the stage for performance and to a range of professionals for mentoring and training. However, not all youth theatres have the luxury of being integral to a professional theatre and the plays in this anthology can be performed in any number of spaces, even outdoors. The most important feature is to provide theatre experiences that are high quality, stimulating, challenging, innovative and fun, enabling children and young people to develop personally, socially and artistically.

The Plays in this anthology

In these four plays, combining both original work with a fresh new adaptation, Rachel offers a concoction of real and imagined observations, predicaments and revelations using themes that resonate and identify strongly to young people; from bullying and anti-social behaviour to breathing contemporary life into Noah, a story from the Bible.

Rocketfuel

Rocketfuel was commissioned for gap year students to perform to secondary school students. The piece is about responsible choices linked to drinking alcohol. The play follows a group of friends as they grow up together. The piece is playful and funny but with a serious core to inspire further discussion.

The humorous and child-like aspects of the first half offer a stark contrast to the more serious elements of the second. Following the story of a group of friends as they grow up together, the piece introduces some playful imagery whilst providing opportunities for a young company to consider how the notion of 'fun' changes throughout adolescence. It looks at risk-taking and the issue of boundaries. How should an individual behave when their peer group is misbehaving? How do teenagers keep themselves safe? What are the likely outcomes of teenagers drinking alcohol? The play will inevitably instigate discussion around the responsibilities of growing up. Rachel's open-ended stage directions present a wonderful opportunity for young people to devise and work creatively on the transition between childhood and young adolescence, using whichever theatrical medium they choose.

LOL (Laughing out loud, crying inside)

LOL was one of Rachel's first ever professional commissions. The brief was to write a piece suitable for Year 9 students to perform to Year 7 students and encourage a conversation about the role of the by-stander in a bullying situation. Once the play had been written, it was sent to secondary schools all around West Sussex. Teachers and young people responded that the subject matter was timely and relevant and it led on to further work in the drama studio and the classroom discussing cyberbullying and online safety.

The play is a short, thought-provoking theatre piece that is particularly suitable for 11 to 14 year olds. The relevance of cyber-bullying in modern society is sensitively but accurately presented and the subject matter lends itself to provocative discussions about human nature and moral responsibility.

Alongside a small number of main characters, the play provides opportunities for an additional group of commentators which adds an interesting dimension /perspective for delivering the narrative taken from the by-stander's viewpoint. There are vast opportunities for discussions and debate and great scope for exploring the issue of cyberbullying and on-line safety through forum theatre techniques.

Three Shoes

Three Shoes is an ambitious play for a large group of mixed age children, which could include adults as well. Spanning 500 years, the play looks at the role of child performers on stage and screen and how the roles they play have changed over time. There are opportunities for dancing, singing, magic, tumbling, in fact whatever the cast is capable of. The play has comedic parts as well as serious ones with the aim of suiting as diverse a cast as possible.

It's an ambitious and unusual play, offering a voice to the young performers whilst presenting their story throughout the course of history. The strong and recurrent imagery offers discussion and debate opportunities around issues that concern young people. The playwright takes a novel approach to the ending by inviting the young performers to add their own ideas and voices at the end of the piece. The play also offers collaborative opportunities for older performers and, consequently, the chance to work cross-generationally, to combine youth or school companies with community groups.

Noah

Noah was a commissioned piece for Chichester Festival Youth Theatre. It provides a brave and uncompromising retelling of the traditional story of the flood, with plenty of humour. There are opportunities for dancing and singing as well as lots of potential for young companies to add as many 'animals' as they like. It offers terrific opportunities for the inclusion of a large cast ensemble and capacity for innovative costume and design elements for the vast array of animals. There is also great scope for new musical composition, for underscoring and for choreographing vibrant dance and movement sequences.

The play was premiered in a temporary theatre space, against the backdrop of Oaklands Park (adjacent to Chichester Festival Theatre). Eighty-six animals stampeded across the park in a spectacular and imaginative movement routine that delighted the eye and was magnificently received by both spectators and critics.

Together, the plays in this anthology offer varied and challenging roles for young people to perform. They offer imaginative opportunities for young people to develop their skills and creativity, gain confidence and learn to work together as a group.

Why join a Youth Theatre?

Young people join youth theatres for various reasons; some with an ambition to pursue a career in the arts, others to widen their social networks and friendship groups, many to develop their confidence and self-esteem. Whatever the reason, participation in youth theatre can have a significant impact, helping young people to develop a strong sense of purpose and direction which can have a profound and far-reaching effect on their lives.

In addition to acquiring knowledge and skills in theatre, other vital and transferrable abilities are also developed – the use of imagination, creativity and self-expression, critical reflection and analysis, an enhanced knowledge of social issues, cultural heritage and aesthetic appreciation. Young people also develop problem solving, self-worth, self-discipline, respect and consideration for others. Equally important is the opportunity to experience fun, the pleasure of social interaction and the excitement of performance.

> *"As well as the opportunity to learn and develop performance skills, youth theatre teaches life skills – building confidence, promoting team work and forging friendships beyond the school playground to name but a few."*
>
> Vicky Edwards, Spirit FM Radio

These crucial attributes flourish through role play, devised work around themes and issues that are important to young people and performances of classical and contemporary drama.

A recent survey into Chichester Festival Youth Theatre's alumni suggests that their participation has given them greater confidence and the ability to communicate and present themselves more effectively in a variety of situations. Youth theatre members understand the importance of commitment, punctuality and the ability to collaborate and work as part of a team. They learn to be good listeners, who are respectful of others people's views and opinions, and ultimately this enriches their positive interaction with the world of work.

> *"I was a very nervous child. When I was a kid, I wasn't confident at all, and then a very close friend of mind got me into the youth theatre, and I got more and more involved. All the friends that I made are still my best friends. We had such a close group. We were doing the shows together, and there was also the social side."*
>
> Actor Mike Slader,
> former Chichester Festival Youth Theatre member

As we celebrate Chichester Festival Youth Theatre's 30th anniversary and my 13th year as Youth Theatre Director, I continue to believe that I have one of the best jobs in the universe – the combination of working in the creative industry with young people! Children and young people have extraordinary imaginations, boundless energy and enthusiasm and an insatiable appetite to soak up and learn about all aspects of theatre – we need to channel, support and nurture these supreme qualities by helping them to achieve their artistic ambitions and talent. It is vital that we continue to inspire and encourage young people from a wide variety of backgrounds, cultures and disciplines to join in the fun, to become active, collaborative and critical members of live theatre.

I thoroughly recommend these plays as a resource for teachers, directors and youth theatre practitioners and hope you'll enjoy working with them as much as we have.

Dale Rooks – Youth Theatre Director,
Chichester Festival Youth Theatre

THE PLAYS

ROCKETFUEL

Commissioned by OnO Theatre company for a schools' tour.

Characters:

Ed

Jenny

Natalie

Olly

Marc

Dez

Bus driver

Security guard

Note: A '/' indicates one character interrupting another.

Scene One: A Playground

Everyone is playing at something – realistic, recognisable playground games. Ed and Jenny are playing at rockets.

ED	Ready for take off?
JENNY	Have we got fuel?
ED	Fill up the tank.
JENNY	Tank filled.
ED	Ready for take off. Counting down/
JENNY	Safety checks?

ED   Safety checks.

JENNY   Good.

ED   Counting down. Ten/

JENNY   Have you strapped in?

ED   You're not my Mum.

JENNY   You still have to strap in.

ED   It's a rocket.

JENNY   Exactly.

ED   Huh?

JENNY   We're going to be travelling at the speed of light. Zooming through the air and then – bursting through our atmosphere – suddenly weightless, floating, dizzy, tingling, buzzing, happy, light-headed, maybe a little bit sick as our stomachs float upwards, giddy, disorientated, and if we're not strapped in we'll just float off into space and we'll be flying, flying, flying/

ED   Strapping in ... Counting down ten, nine, eight/

JENNY   Errr.

ED   What Jenny?

JENNY   Have you shut the door?

ED   Of course I've shut the door.

JENNY   And activated the seal?

ED   And activated the seal.

JENNY   And the airlock?

ED   I've had enough.

JENNY   And packed the space food?

ED   Play on your own.

JENNY   Just a bit of attention to detail. Got to be safe. It's risky enough going into space. Got to be careful.

ED   I'm going to play with Marc.

JENNY   No. Don't go. Sorry. Sorry. Sorry. Sorry ... All checks complete ... Commencing countdown. Go on. Please Ed. Commencing countdown.

ED   Whatever – commencing countdown. Ten, nine, eight, seven, six/

JENNY   Ah?

ED   Jenny ...

JENNY   Nothing. Sorry.

ED   Five, four, three, two, one, blastoff!

Jenny and Ed take off in their imaginary rocket and fly around the playground. Focus shifts to Natalie and Marc. Jenny and Ed keep flying, possibly fighting some aliens as they go.

MARC   I dare you.

NATALIE   You can dare him if you like. Doesn't mean he's going to do it.

OLLY   It's OK Natalie ... I like climbing trees.

NATALIE   Don't do it Olly. You'll fall out and kill yourself and then Mum'll kill you. It's too high.

MARC   Scared?

OLLY   Course not. I've climbed way bigger trees than this.

NATALIE   No you haven't.

OLLY   Shut up Nat ... I'm brilliant at climbing trees. Love it. Great buzz.

MARC   My brother's climbed this tree loads.

NATALIE   Yes. But your brother's an idiot. And he's older.

MARC   So?

NATALIE   Longer arms ... Like a stupid monkey.

MARC   I'm going to get him to get you.

NATALIE   Scary.

MARC   Dez. Dez. Get over here.

Dez lumbers over.

DEZ   What's up?

MARC   I've dared Olly to climb the tree – and he's scared.

DEZ   I climb that tree loads. It's dead easy. Well – easy to be dead. Unless you're me.

MARC   He's chicken.

OLLY   I'm not.

NATALIE   We're not allowed to climb trees. What if the teacher sees?

OLLY   So?

MARC   I dare you.

OLLY   So?

MARC   I triple donkey double donut dare you with no returns.

OLLY   Oh.

DEZ   Well, Olly my little man – you have to do it now. Go on.

NATALIE   It doesn't mean anything.

OLLY   It does Nat ... It's the triple donkey double donut dare. It means EVERYTHING.

MARC   Well? Are you doing it or not? Or are you scared? Are you a chicken? Well? ... Make up your mind Olly.

DEZ   I think he's chicken.

MARC   Me too.

OLLY   I am not chicken.

Olly starts to climb the tree. Ed and Jenny come over to watch.

OLLY	This is easy.
DEZ	Told you.

He gets stuck.

NATALIE	Are you OK?
OLLY	I'm fine.
JENNY	You're quite high.
OLLY	I'm fine.
ED	You don't look fine.
OLLY	I'm fine.
DEZ	I think he's stuck.
MARC	I do too.
OLLY	I'm fine.
MARC	Well, move then.
OLLY	I'm stuck.

NATALIE I knew it ... What if someone sees? Can't you just come down?

MARC If you come down now you'll be the biggest loser ever.

OLLY I don't want to come down. Ed. Jenny. Go and distract the teacher.

JENNY How?

OLLY I don't know. Go and behave like idiots near him – it shouldn't be too hard.

ED I resent that.

NATALIE Just go. Please. Oh no oh no oh no.

Ed and Jenny go.

ED   Back in the rocket.

They zoom off round the teacher, distracting him.

MARC   I knew you couldn't do it. You're useless.

NATALIE   Why are you so mean?

MARC   Because your brother's got stuck up a tree and I knew he would. Only my brother can climb this tree properly ... And me/

OLLY   I think I can make it up to the next branch.

NATALIE   It doesn't look very strong, Olly ... Can't you just come down again?

OLLY   I don't want to come down again. I want to climb this tree.

MARC   Just give up you big loser.

OLLY   I am not a loser ... I can do it ... I think. I can do it.

He overreaches, stumbles but doesn't fall. A moment.

NATALIE *(to audience)* He can't do it.

MARC *(to audience)* He can't do it.

DEZ *(to audience)* He can't do it.

OLLY   OK. Maybe I can't do it ... *(Takes a moment)* I'm coming down.

NATALIE   Good.

MARC   I knew it. You big loser. Wimp. Chicken.

OLLY   Shut up. I did it. I went well high ... If I'd have gone to that next branch I'd have fallen ... I'm not an idiot. I've got football club this afternoon. I don't want to break anything. I'm playing centre forward.

He starts making his way down. Ed and Jenny come back over.

ED   Did you do it?

OLLY	Yep.
ED	Cool.
JENNY	Well done.
MARC	Hardly.
ED	What?
MARC	He didn't climb the tree.
JENNY	I don't understand.

NATALIE   Olly did it. He climbed the tree, he came down before he hurt himself. He's my brother and I'm proud of him.

OLLY	Shut up Nat.
NATALIE	Shut up Olly.
MARC	He didn't climb the tree.
JENNY	Look. I'm confused. Did he climb the tree or not?
MARC	Not.
OLLY	Did.

MARC   Look. If you're going to climb a tree properly then you have to get to the top.

NATALIE	He went as high as he could.
MARC	Well, it wasn't high enough.

OLLY   You think you can go higher? Be my guest ... Go on Marc – you're so brave – show us how it's done. Show us what your 'amazing' big brother can do. Go on Dez. Or go on Marc. Show us how much fun it is breaking your legs. You think it's worth taking the risk. Be my guest. I'm not an idiot.

ED	Go on.
JENNY	Go on.
NATALIE	Yeah. Go on.
OLLY	Shut up, Natalie.

ED   Go on Marc. Climb the tree.

JENNY   Go on then.

A long pause.

MARC   Footie anyone?

General agreement.

MARC   Not you ... You're rubbish.

NATALIE   But I/

OLLY   Just ignore her ... Natalie – please stop hanging round. Mum said/

ED   Come on then. Olly, you can be captain.

They divide into teams and play.

NATALIE   It's not fair.

MARC   Get over it.

NATALIE   Why can't I play?

ED   The teams wouldn't be even.

MARC   You're a girl.

NATALIE   So's Jenny.

MARC   Yes. But she's good at football.

JENNY   She could play, couldn't she?

OLLY/MARC/ED No.

JENNY   Sorry, Nat.

They play.

MARC   Loser. Couldn't even climb a tree.

JENNY   I thought he did climb the tree.

OLLY   I did.

MARC	Not properly. Loser.
OLLY	Well, you were too scared to even try.
MARC	Shut up.

Marc does a dirty tackle on Olly.

Olly is down – hurt drama queen/ premier footballer style.

OLLY	What did you do that for?
ED	Get up, captain.
OLLY	It really hurts.
MARC	Stop making a fuss.
ED	That was a dirty move Marc.
MARC	Whatever.
JENNY	I think it's broken.
ED	Shall we get a teacher?
OLLY	No.
NATALIE	I think we'd better.
OLLY	It's fine.
JENNY	That was a dirty tackle.
NATALIE	You can't even stand on it.

MARC   Go on then. Run and tell a teacher. You big bunch of losers. If you tell on me I'll get my brother to beat you all up.

ED	I'm not going.
JENNY	I ...
OLLY	Nat. Don't go. *(A moment.)*

NATALIE   I'm not scared of your stupid brother. I'm telling ... And you are going to get in so much trouble. Come on Olly. Your foot's swelling up like a balloon.

Nat helps Olly hobble away.

MARC	Why am I the one getting in trouble?
ED	Climbing the tree.
MARC	I didn't make him.
ED	You triple donkey double donut dared him.
JENNY	And you broke his ankle.
MARC	He'll be OK ... He was just being a wimp ... Who's in goal?
JENNY	I don't feel like playing.
ED	Back to the rocket?
JENNY	Why not?

Ed and Jenny return to their rocket. Marc is left alone. He tries not to look lonely.

Scene Two: On the Bus

BUS DRIVER Can you all sit down quietly? I am not going to ask you again.

General mayhem.

NATALIE *(narration)* He asked us again. He always asked us again. Every morning of every weekday of every school week of every year we went to school.

BUS DRIVER I am not going to ask you again. Can you all PLEASE sit down – quietly.

NATALIE *(narration)* See.

BUS DRIVER I am not going to move this bus until you are all sitting down quietly.

MARC Good. 'Cos we don't want to go to school anyway.

NATALIE *(narration)* Not exactly true. Not exactly not true. It depended on the day, it depended on the year, it depended on what was waiting for us at school – what lessons, what friends. But one thing was always the same. Every day. Year in. Year out.

BUS DRIVER WILL YOU ALL JUST SIT DOWN? WHAT IF I HAVE TO STOP THE BUS SUDDENLY? I'M NOT ASKING YOU TO SIT DOWN FOR MY OWN ENTERTAINMENT. IT'S NOT SAFE, YOU STUPID KIDS. SIT THE BLOOMING HECK DOWN, WILL YOU?

NATALIE *(narration)* See.

Time passes. We see the children growing up a bit. This could be done through dance or movement.

JENNY	So. Party tonight. Who's coming?
MARC	'Course.
ED	Maybe.
OLLY	Yep.
JENNY	Nat?
NATALIE	Dunno. Maybe. Depends ... Ed?
OLLY	What's it matter if he's going? You know you're going.
NATALIE	Well you're not ... You're grounded.
OLLY	That was last week.
MARC	Grounded. Ha!
NATALIE	Shut up Marc.
ED	Well, if we're going, what're we going to take?
JENNY	Oh yeah.
OLLY	What?

ED   Well. We can't just go with nothing. We'll look like right idiots ... We need to take something ... something cool ... like beer or WKD or Bacardi Breezers or something.

JENNY   I haven't got anything. And I don't have any money.

ED   I don't either.

OLLY   Nope.

JENNY   Do your parents have anything you could take?

OLLY   No.

NATALIE   You know he's grounded 'cos he tried to nick a tenner from mum's purse. Idiot.

MARC   Grounded. Ha!

OLLY   Shut up Marc.

MARC   Well I'm going to get something off my brother to take. He's got loads of stuff.

NATALIE   Oh yeah – the wonderful Dez. How's he doing? Got an ASBO yet? Loser.

JENNY   Mum'll never give me anything. And she doesn't have any booze in the house anyway.

ED   Well, we need to take something ... I wanna get drunk tonight.

OLLY   Me too.

ED   I just want a nice chilled out evening. Bit of fun. Some beers. That nice warm tingling feeling. A bit light-headed. Just chilled. Not masses. Just, you know, that nice drunk feeling.

NATALIE   Tipsy.

ED   More than tipsy, less than paralytic.

OLLY   I wanna get ratted.

NATALIE   Chilled is good. Just a bit relaxed.

JENNY   So what are we going to do? We can't buy anything anyway – we're too young and that fake ID Ed got looks rubbish.

ED   No, it doesn't.

JENNY   Ed. Seriously. The man in the photo has a moustache – you can't even grow fluff on your stupid babyface chin.

OLLY   So what are we going to do?

NATALIE   Ed and me had an idea.

ED   Tell them.

NATALIE   No. You tell.

ED   After school. Let's go down the shops. You know the one with a well dozy security guard.

JENNY   Yeah?

NATALIE   Well, we think, if we time it right, one of us can get into the off-licence and take a bottle of something and he'll never know.

JENNY   Really?

OLLY   No way.

NATALIE   What? It's a good idea.

MARC   You lot? You'd get caught in seconds.

OLLY   I don't like it.

ED   Well, we can't go to the party without taking something cool. Otherwise no one will talk to us.

JENNY   There's gonna be Year 9 girls there.

NATALIE   They don't even know Olly's born.

OLLY   They do. One of them dropped her bag the other day and I did the gentlemanly thing and picked it up for her and she smiled at me and said thanks and then invited me to this party.

NATALIE   You're like a puppy dog really, aren't you? A big soppy puppy dog with dopey soft brown eyes.

OLLY   Shut up, Nat.

NATALIE   Shut up, Olly.

MARC   I'm going out with a Year 10 girl.

OLLY   No, you aren't.

MARC   I am.

OLLY   Who?

MARC   She's from a different school.

OLLY   'Course she is.

NATALIE   Anyway. Come on. Let's go round the shops after school. Who's in?

ED   Me.

JENNY   Me.

NATALIE   Brilliant ... We need to come up with a proper plan.

OLLY   Nat? Seriously? What if Mum/

NATALIE   Shut up Olly ... You're embarrassing me.

OLLY   Well, I'm not going.

ED   Go on. Come with us. It'll be a laugh ... And you're the tallest. We need someone tall.

OLLY   Why? No you don't ... And I don't appreciate you getting my sister involved in this stuff ... Natalie/

ED   It was her idea.

NATALIE   I can make my own mind up, Olly.

OLLY   I'll tell Mum.

NATALIE   Then I'll tell her about /

OLLY   OK. Fine. Fine. I won't say anything.

NATALIE   Good.

ED   So are you coming?

OLLY   I suppose.

ED   Marc?

MARC   Whatever.

ED   Good ...

JENNY *(narration)* School went so slowly that day. I never knew time could even go that slowly. We were all thinking the same thing. Thinking about the party. Thinking about the shop. Thinking about all those drinks lined up. The light glinting off every curve of every glass bottle. Wondering which one we were going to try and hide in our coat pocket. Wondering who'd be brave enough. Who'd dare who. Who'd try and impress who. Legging it afterwards. All day my legs were tight with anticipation. Ready to run. Ready to steal a bottle of booze and run the fastest I'd ever run before. Ready ...

ALL   Ready.

Suddenly everyone's running in different directions. Shouting. Chaotic. Over the chaos, shouts of:

Come on. Hurry up. That's the shop. Ready?

I dare you.

Are you chicken?

Go on.

Now.

He's not looking.

Just grab one.

Oh no.

He's seen us.

Run.

Here.

Catch.

Not me.

Not me.

Run.

Run.

Run.

RUN.

Natalie is left with the bottle.

Scene Three: Security Guard's Office

Everyone looking very dejected.

OLLY   Great idea, Ed.

JENNY   We're in really big trouble, aren't we? What a nightmare.

MARC   Shut up, Jenny.

ED   Well, why didn't you all run away?

OLLY   We tried. We didn't know there were two of them ... You didn't say there were two of them.

JENNY   We are in so much trouble. This is all your fault Natalie ... And you Ed.

NATALIE   You didn't have to come.

MARC   Look. It's not like the door's locked. Let's just leg it.

NATALIE   Don't be stupid. What about CCTV? They said they'd call the police if we ran away.

JENNY   He'll probably call the police anyway.

ED   Did anyone actually get anything?

OLLY   No.

JENNY	Nothing.
MARC	Wasn't trying anyway.
OLLY	What about you Ed?
ED	I got a *Twix*.
OLLY	A *Twix*?
ED	Nat said she wanted some chocolate.
NATALIE	Did you know they're my favourite?
OLLY	Ed, mate, stop hitting on my sister. It's disgusting.
MARC	So is that all? Just one lousy *Twix*. You lot/
NATALIE	Not just a *Twix* ... *(She produces a bottle of whisky)*

MARC Whisky! I can't believe we're going to get in trouble over a bottle of whisky. That is so not cool. It's like the stuff my grandpa drinks ... That's old person drink ... Couldn't you have taken something cooler? We can hardly turn up to the party with that.

NATALIE	Well, thank you very much. Like you did any better.
OLLY	Natalie ... I can't believe you. You're in so much trouble.
NATALIE	I know. I think he saw me anyway.
ED	Don't worry about it – it'll be OK.
NATALIE	Yeah?
OLLY	You'll have to give it back.
NATALIE	I know.
MARC	What a bunch of losers.
JENNY	Well, why do you hang round with us?
OLLY	He doesn't have any other friends.
NATALIE	Shh. I can hear him coming back.
ED	Quick give me the bottle.
NATALIE	But/

ED   Just give it.

Ed grabs the bottle. They nervously await the opening of the door.

OLLY *(narration)* Marc's right. We are a bunch of losers. Getting caught straight away, the very first time we try something like this. We all sit there in the office. Heads bowed. Ashamed. I can tell Natalie's about to cry – she's doing that thing she does – she did it when she was five and she still does it now. No one knows what to do. But then Ed ...

As the Guard comes in:

ED   Sir. 'Scuse me. But ... Can you let all my friends go? ... It was my idea. Only me. I'm the one who stole the stuff. They tried to tell me not to. I just did it because there's this party and /

GUARD   There's always a party.

ED   And I've never done anything like this before. But I feel really bad. I made all my friends come even though they didn't want to. It's not fair if they all get in trouble.

GUARD   I don't know.

ED   Seriously. Please. None of us has ever been in trouble. It's all my fault. They just stayed because they're my mates.

GUARD   Really?

General mute pleading and nodding.

ED   Please. We're really sorry. I'm really sorry. They shouldn't get in trouble because of me ... Look. Here's the whisky. It's not damaged. Please just let them go.

GUARD   I shouldn't really ... My boss.

ED   One form instead of five. One address. One phone call. Seriously, sir ... please.

GUARD   You kids are too young to start messing around with this nonsense. Stealing. Stealing alcohol – it's not funny.

You're too young even to be drinking it. What were you thinking of? ... Go on then. I can't be bothered with all the paperwork ... I don't understand it – you all seem like nice enough kids ... Go on. Scram ... And don't let me catch you doing anything like this again or else ... or else ... Oh whatever. Go on ... Hop it you lot ... And don't let me see you round here again.

NATALIE   I ...

JENNY   Well ...

ED   It's OK. I'll see you later.

MARC   Let's just go.

OLLY   Come on Nat ... Natalie. Leave it.

NATALIE   But ...

OLLY   Come on.

The others go.

ED   Here. I'm really sorry ... It was only meant to be a laugh.

He gives back the whisky.

GUARD   I should call the police.

ED   Please don't ... I absolutely completely swear I'll never do anything like this again.

GUARD   You stole something from a shop ... It's not a joke.

ED   But I gave it back.

GUARD   That's not the point.

ED   I know ... I wish I'd never done it.

GUARD   Well. What am I going to do with you now?

ED   Please. Sir. Don't call the police.

A moment.

Scene Four: The Park

JENNY   We shouldn't have left him.

NATALIE   Poor Ed.

MARC   I'm cold.

OLLY   If he doesn't hurry up we're never going to get to this party.

NATALIE   Is that all you can think about?

OLLY   Well, that's been the reason for all of this stupid rubbish. I just wanted, you know, a good night. A good party. You know, getting wasted. Getting completely and utterly wasted. I was really looking forward to it.

JENNY   Even the hangover?

OLLY   Yeah. Even the hangover.

JENNY   Weirdo. Swollen head. Carpet tongue. Who looks forward to that?

OLLY   I just wanted a really good night.

NATALIE   Will he know where to come find us?

JENNY   Of course he'll know.

OLLY   I wish he'd hurry up.

JENNY   Is that him?

NATALIE   Yeah ... ED, ED, OVER HERE.

OLLY   He can see us. You don't need to shout your head off.

Ed joins them.

NATALIE   Ed. You're my hero.

OLLY   Stop it Nat.

JENNY   What happened?

ED   It was fine. I told him how much I liked his cap and that I want to be a security guard just like him when I grow up and he said, 'You're like the son I never had.' And then he hugged me, like this, and then he cried. And then he hugged me again.

Ed hugs Olly.

OLLY   Get off.

NATALIE   Really?

ED   Nah ... We're not allowed back near the shop and he called my Mum – she sounded like she was about to take off, she was so cross. I was meant to go straight home ... Oh well.

MARC   Did you keep the whisky?

ED   No, I gave it back.

MARC   Loser.

ED   I kept the *Twix* though ... Here.

He gives it to Natalie.

NATALIE   Thanks Ed. Mmmmm. Stolen chocolate. Yum. You're like Robin Hood.

OLLY   You should give it back.

ED   What?

NATALIE   What?

OLLY   I can't believe you'd just eat chocolate that someone stole.

NATALIE   You would.

OLLY   Yeah, but/

NATALIE   What's it matter?

OLLY   Up to you ... Your conscience/

ED   What's the problem? They only cost like 60p. No one cares.

OLLY   Then you should have bought one. Just 'cos it's cheap doesn't mean it's not still stealing.

JENNY   Yeah. Whatever Olly ... Give us a bit Nat ... I'm starving.

NATALIE   What's your problem, Olly? Seriously? Whatever.

Natalie shares the chocolate. Pointedly not giving Olly any.

OLLY   So. What are we going to do?

JENNY   What about?

OLLY   This party idiot ... We still haven't got anything to take. And/

ED   ... Marc ... Your brother ...?

MARC   What about him?

ED   Could he help us out?

MARC   Why should he?

NATALIE   Look, Ed helped you out.

MARC   Fine. Whatever.

OLLY *(narration)* So Marc called his brother. And we waited. Ed and Natalie making gooey eyes at each other thinking no one else could see them. Jenny hung about. Marc didn't say anything to anyone – as always. And I just kept watching the park gate – waiting for Marc's brother to turn up. And I watched. And I waited. And time kept slipping away and I just imagined that great party going on in that Year 9 girl's house, that we had an actual invitation to, that we were missing. We're missing the party. We're missing the party. We're missing the party.

Dez arrives.

DEZ   Alright kids. I understand my services are required.

MARC   Cheers.

He throws a can of something towards Marc.

MARC   That's better.

DEZ   Do your friends want a drink then?

MARC   I should imagine so.

DEZ   Here you go then, kids.

ED   You don't need to call us kids. You're only a bit older than us.

OLLY   Is that all you brought? Like eleven cans of lager and a bottle of something without a label on it that smells like paint? We can't turn up to the party with that, can we? What a joke.

JENNY   Chill Olly.

OLLY   Right. That's it. We're not going, are we? We're not going to the party. What a complete waste of energy.

JENNY   Look. It's a nice evening. Let's just sit here and have a drink and forget about it ... Those Year 9 girls don't know you're born anyway. They're all going out with boys in Year 11.

DEZ   Do you want my booze or not?

OLLY *(narration)* He had us there. We did want his booze. Of course we did. So we smiled at him through gritted teeth and drank his nasty cheap beer and the strange stuff that burnt on the way down and then made you feel warm inside and before long we were all feeling a bit more relaxed and a bit ... merrier.

Everyone is a bit drunk and giggly.

OLLY   You know what, right, I'm going to go up to her in school and say, 'I'm sorry I missed your party but you're the most beautiful girl in the whole world.' And then I'm going to kiss her. In front of everyone. Even though she's in Year 9.

NATALIE   No you aren't ... And if you did she'd probably slap you ... You're so drunk.

JENNY   I think it's sweet.

ED   What would you do if I said that to you, Natalie?

OLLY	If you kiss my sister I'll punch you in the face.
NATALIE	Why do you care?
OLLY	'Cos you're my sister.
JENNY	Don't fight. Look. It's a beautiful evening.
ED	I want to fly to the moon.
JENNY	How much have you had to drink?
ED	Enough to want to fly to the moon.
JENNY	No. Really. Ed. How much?
ED	Dunno. Lost count. Couple of beers and a load of that stuff.
JENNY	What is that stuff? ... Dez?
DEZ	This my dear is *White Lightning* – a most particularly unpleasant brew of apples and alcohol – the best way of getting rat-arsed if you're fourteen, sat in a park, and have acne, B.O. and no girlfriend.
JENNY	It's disgusting.
ED	I like it.
JENNY	You're wasted.
ED	I'm happy. I feel like I'm flying ... I feel a bit mental. Come on.
JENNY	Fly to the moon with me.
JENNY	In our rocket? Remember? Our rocket.
ED	Come on then.
JENNY	Ready for take off?
ED	We need fuel.
JENNY	We got fuel.
OLLY	That's beer.
JENNY	It's rocket fuel.

ED   Rocket fuel.

JENNY   It's such a BEAUTIFUL evening.

Ed and Jenny recreate the rocket from the first scene. Amusing. Unsteady. They 'fly' around, fighting aliens, etc.

NATALIE *(narration)* It was. A beautiful evening. I'd never noticed how beautiful the park was. The trees were beautiful. The grass was beautiful. The swings were beautiful. I felt so happy. So alive. So – sort of – floaty. I wanted to share it with someone. I looked around for Ed. I wanted to share it all with Ed. I love Ed. I want to tell him that I ... But when I turned round – Marc was right there.

Marc is right there, suddenly they're kissing.

Ed notices.

Olly notices.

Jenny holds Olly back.

JENNY   A little help here?

ED   Whatever.

Natalie and Marc stop kissing.

NATALIE *(narration)* I don't know why I did that ... I wish I hadn't.

Jenny can't hold Olly anymore. He launches himself at Marc.

OLLY   Get your filthy hands off my sister.

DEZ   Aw. Look at the little boys. Fight. Come on Marc. I've taught you better than this. Go under. Uppercut. Right hook. Go on little bro'. Hit him.

JENNY   Can't you help me stop them?

DEZ   This is far more fun. They look like such cute little idiots.

NATALIE   Olly. Leave it ... Ed ... I ...

NATALIE *(narration)* And suddenly the evening isn't quite so beautiful anymore.

OLLY   I dare someone to climb that tree.

NATALIE   Olly. No. It's way too high.

OLLY   Go on. Marc. Climb that tree. Or are you chicken?

MARC   Don't want to.

OLLY   I triple donkey double donut dare you with no returns.

JENNY AND ED   Ooooooh.

ED   What you gonna do, Marc?

JENNY   Go on, Marc.

MARC   I could climb that tree easy.

NATALIE   No you couldn't.

He wobbles.

JENNY   Have some more rocket fuel.

ED   Dez? Give him some more rocket fuel.

DEZ   It's beer, you saddos.

MARC   Give us another can, Dez.

DEZ   Whatever.

NATALIE   Haven't we had enough?

MARC   ... Right.

He hesitates.

OLLY   Scared?

ED   Chicken?

NATALIE   Marc – you can't climb that tree.

He drinks some more.

JENNY   Houston, he's tanked up and ready for lift off.

MARC   Someone give me a leg up.

He's climbing the tree and is suddenly more animated than we've seen him before.

MARC   I'm doing a lot better than any of you. See. I'm like a monkey. I'm like Superman. I've got super-strength and super-swingyness. Look at me. Wheeee. I'm unbreakable. I'm going to climb to the stars. Not like you in your stupid pretend rocket. Wow. It's so beautiful up here. Someone throw me another beer.

NATALIE   You've made your point. Can you come down now? You're too far up ... You're too drunk.

MARC   No, I'm not. I'm going to live up here forever. Like a monkey.

He swings between the branches.

JENNY   Marc. Come down ... Olly. Tell him.

OLLY   OK. You've made your point, come down now.

ED   Come down.

General 'come down' encouragement.

Suddenly, he falls.

Natalie screams.

OLLY   What do we do?

NATALIE   He's dead, isn't he? He's dead. He's dead. He's dead.

ED   This is your fault, Olly.

OLLY   How is it my fault?

ED   You dared him.

DEZ   Can you all stop panicking and can someone call an ambulance?

OLLY   They'll call the police. We'll be sent to prison.

NATALIE   I'm calling.

OLLY   This is all my fault.

NATALIE   I should never have kissed him.

JENNY   I shouldn't have given him the beer.

ED   I called him chicken. Why did I do that?

Siren in the distance.

JENNY   The noise. Oh God, my head … I'm going to be sick.

OLLY   Look at it. Kids. In the park. After dark. Beer cans everywhere. It looks bad.

ED   We should tell them/

OLLY   Tell them what?

ED   This isn't us. We're not really like this. We're good. We're the good kids. Sensible. Clever.

NATALIE   Yeah. Really clever … Our friend's dead or something.

ED   Usually. Good. Sensible. Clever.

JENNY   My head.

OLLY   I'm gonna be sick.

NATALIE   Look at the way he's lying there.

ED   What are we going to do?

The sirens get closer.

In the distance we hear a rocket taking off and an echo of the children's countdown from earlier.

The friends look at each other, paralysed with fear.

Lights down.

The end.

LOL (LAUGHING OUT LOUD, CRYING INSIDE)

For *Anti-Bullying Week* 2006. Commissioned by West Sussex Community Safety Team. Performed in schools across West Sussex.

Characters:

The Girls

Elly – Friends with Izz and Suze. Lives next door to Izz.

Amy – Going out with Dan. Ben's sister. Lives next door to Rob.

Suze – Friends with Izz and Elly. Going out with Rob.

Izz – Friends with Suze and Elly. Lives next door to Elly.

The Boys

Dan – Amy's boyfriend. Friends with Andrew.

Rob – Going out with Suze. Friends with Ben. Lives next door to Ben and Amy.

Ben – Amy's brother. Fancies Elly. Friends with, and lives next door to Rob.

Andrew – Friends with Dan.

The Others *(these two roles can be split between more than two people)*

Commentator 1 / Commentator 2 – Setting the scene. Observing and commenting on the drama. Asking the audience questions. Challenging.

Note: A '/' indicates an interruption.

Scene One: Monday

The bus stop – Suze and Izz are waiting for the Number 26 bus. The two Commentators are watching. It is drizzling so they are holding umbrellas. They talk to the audience.

COMMENTATOR 1 The bus stop. Monday morning.

COMMENTATOR 2 Always seems to be raining.

COMMENTATOR 1 Recovering from the weekend.

COMMENTATOR 2 Seeing whose tag is fresh on the bus shelter this week.

COMMENTATOR 1 And whether the glass has survived since last Friday ... or is lying around us like crystallised raindrops – until the council bothers to send someone to replace it again.

COMMENTATOR 2 Waiting for the bus to arrive – the stinking, dirty, noisy, flea-infested bus ...

COMMENTATOR 1 ... driven by the most miserable man in the whole county.

COMMENTATOR 2 There's ten of us who wait at this bus stop ... nothing much in common ... But we all catch the bus to school from the stop outside the *Pig and Whistle* on the Avenue.

COMMENTATOR 1 And somehow that's enough.

COMMENTATOR 2 We live near each other.

COMMENTATOR 1 Our parents know each other.

COMMENTATOR 2 Our brothers and sisters know each other.

COMMENTATOR 1 We know each other ...

SUZE   Where's Elly? She'll miss the bus.

IZZ   Where were you this weekend? You weren't even online.

SUZE   Mum and me were rowing so she grounded me and now I'm not allowed to use the computer. She's well out of order.

IZZ   You know on Friday afternoon Elly was looking all ... you know ...

SUZE   Yeah?

IZZ   Well, turns out she was in the loos and Amy and some others broke the toilet door down and filmed Elly having a wee ...

SUZE   No way.

IZZ   Yeah. And then Amy posted it online at the weekend ... cos she's mad with Elly about Elly calling her a tart or something, even though she so *is* one, and then everyone was messaging and texting about it ... I texted you ...

SUZE   Your message didn't make sense and I've got no credit and I'm broke *(Reads from her phone)* 'Lk @ A's fbk. Mntl!!! LOL' ... I mean ... How am I meant to understand that?

IZZ   Suze you are like the only person in the world who still doesn't understand text-speak.

SUZE   So has everyone seen it, other than me, then?

IZZ   I guess so.

SUZE   Typical ... I'll bloody kill my mum ... What's it like? Is it bad?

IZZ   Yeah.

SUZE   Really?

IZZ   Yeah ...

SUZE   What can you see?

IZZ   Everything ... the worst thing is ...

SUZE   Yeah ...

IZZ   I'll tell you later.

SUZE   Izz!

IZZ   Shhh ... Hey Elly.

Elly comes to join the queue.

SUZE   Hiya.

IZZ   Good weekend?

ELLY   What do you think?

Amy, Dan and Andrew come to join the queue. They ignore Izz, Elly and Suze. Amy and Dan are smooching.

AMY   I missed you so much, babe.

DAN   I only saw you last night ...

AMY   Yeah ... That was ... fun ...

IZZ   Ugh. Get a room.

AMY   Got a problem?

IZZ   I just had my breakfast ... don't want to see it again, quite yet, thank you.

AMY   Well, I wouldn't look in the mirror then ... minger.

IZZ   Cow.

ELLY   Leave it, Izz.

AMY   Oh you're here, are you? Wet yourself much over the weekend?

Dan and Andrew laugh. Rob and Ben rush up.

AMY   If you'd missed the bus again Mum would have killed you.

BEN   Only if you'd told her.

SUZE   Hi Rob.

ROB   Hi babe ... What happened to you this weekend?

SUZE   Got grounded ... wasn't allowed to use the computer/

ANDREW   Aw, what a shame ... the princess wasn't allowed to play with her toys ...

ROB   Shut it, Andy.

ANDREW   Whatever.

DAN   Hey Elly ... Heard from any agents yet? You've definitely got a future in the film industry. Oh, did I say 'film'? ... I meant 'Porn .'

IZZ   Don't let them get to you.

ELLY   I want to die.

SUZE   Just ignore them.

BEN   Hey Elly.

IZZ   Leave her alone, weirdo.

BEN   I was just saying hello.

IZZ   Whatever ...

COMMENTATOR 1 And then,

COMMENTATOR 2 The bus arrives.

COMMENTATOR 1 And then,

COMMENTATOR 2 As Elly gets on the bus,

COMMENTATOR 1 There is a brief moment of silence ...

COMMENTATOR 2 Before a whisper turns into a hum turns into a chant turns into a shout turns into howling, howling laughter.

COMMENTATOR 1 Poor Elly.

COMMENTATOR 2 Poor Elly.

Scene Two: Tuesday

The schoolyard – before school. The Commentators are throwing a football around.

COMMENTATOR 1 Tuesday.

COMMENTATOR 2 The square of concrete that is, laughably, referred to as/

COMMENTATOR 1 The Playground.

COMMENTATOR 2 Though no-one ever really 'plays' here.

They throw the ball away.

COMMENTATOR 1 Before school.

COMMENTATOR 2 A time to finish off last night's homework.

COMMENTATOR 1 A time to lean against a wall and practice looking fierce.

COMMENTATOR 2 A time to try to become invisible ...

Andrew, Dan and Amy are leaning against a wall.

AMY ... Did you see her face in Maths yesterday? When everyone just started going 'ssssss' really quietly ... Miss didn't know what was going on – but Elly did.

DAN Wicked.

AMY It's had about a thousand hits already. Everyone in the whole school must have seen it.

DAN You're amazing, babes.

AMY And you should see some of the comments – mental!

ANDREW That's ...

AMY What? What's up Andrew? You got something to say?

ANDREW Just. You've made your point. Give it a rest now.

AMY Aw. Are you feeling bad about poor Weeface? Are you in love with her?

ANDREW Get lost.

DAN Andrew loves Weeface. Andrew loves Weeface.

ANDREW Whatever.

Andrew goes. Izz, Suze, Elly and Rob walk past. Dan and Amy taunt Elly.

DAN   Weeface.

SUZE   Just ignore them.

ELLY   It's not just them though, is it? It's the whole school.

IZZ   It'll blow over. It's nothing. They're just being stupid.

ELLY   Did you see the blog? Everyone's laughing at me. Everyone hates me.

AMY   Weeface …

COMMENTATOR 1 It could go on like this for quite a while.

COMMENTATOR 2 Insults and jeering.

COMMENTATOR 1 Elly slowly crumbling inside.

COMMENTATOR 2 And no-one really doing anything about it.

COMMENTATOR 1 But what should they do?

COMMENTATOR 2 What would *you* do?

Scene Three: Wednesday

The lunch hall. The Commentators are holding lunch trays.

COMMENTATOR 1 Wednesday.

COMMENTATOR 2 Half-way through the week. Half-way through the day.

COMMENTATOR 1 Thank God.

COMMENTATOR 2 The dining room.

COMMENTATOR 1 Noisy. Smelly. Greasy.

COMMENTATOR 2 They're killing us with this food. I saw it on the telly – it's a conspiracy.

COMMENTATOR 1 It's 'cos it's all crap.

COMMENTATOR 2 But it tastes good.

COMMENTATOR 1 So don't complain.

COMMENTATOR 2 Well, don't blame me when you're too fat to move and your arteries clog up and you die …

Everyone is in the queue except Elly and Amy.

BEN	Where's Elly?
SUZE	Why should you care?
BEN	I … I just …
SUZE	She's not in school.
IZZ	Do you know what happened last night?
ROB	I do.

Rob and Suze giggle and cuddle.

IZZ Ugh. Get a room … Elly started getting these text messages. Horrid ones. She was round mine and she got a text and her face just went, like, grey. That cow has posted Elly's mobile number under the video and now loads of weirdoes and freaks are texting her. And some of them are really nasty and threatening stuff … Elly is completely freaked out. She got her Mum to let her stay home today, said she was sick …

BEN	So what are you going to do?
IZZ	Me?
BEN	This is out of control. Someone should do something.
SUZE	It's not our business.

IZZ This stuff happens. Best just to keep your head down … Be pleased it's not you.

ANDREW	Alright?
IZZ	Don't you talk to us.
ANDREW	Look. I'm through with Amy and her lot. She's well out of order.
BEN	Maybe I should talk to Mum.
SUZE	What planet are you living on?
IZZ	It'll just make it worse.
SUZE	Elly should never have called Amy a slut ... she's just got to deal with it now.

BEN *(to the commentators)* And what about you two? Standing there. Watching everything. What about you?

COMMENTATOR 1 It's none of our business.

COMMENTATOR 2 Nothing to do with us.

COMMENTATOR 1 We don't know any of you lot.

COMMENTATOR 2 Not that we don't care.

COMMENTATORS 1 and **2** But it's not our problem.

BEN	Oi. Dan. Daniel!
DAN	What is it?
BEN	This thing between Amy and Elly – it's going too far.
DAN	Amy's cool.
BEN	I don't get it.

DAN Elly's so lame ... 'Oh no, don't film me doing a wee – wahhhhh.' She's got to sort it herself. It's good for her ... toughen her up a bit ... Look Ben, if you're so bothered then tell a teacher, why don't you?

ALL *(other than Ben)* Tell tale tit. You smell like shit. Tell another tale and your arse will split. Tell tale tit. You smell like shit. Tell another tale and your arse will split.

They repeat as a whisper as the Commentators address the audience.

COMMENTATOR 1 And then the first of them reaches the point of the queue where we must choose between chips ... or chips.

COMMENTATOR 2 And so the bickering stops.

COMMENTATOR 1 For the moment.

COMMENTATOR 2 Any salad?

COMMENTATOR 1 Don't push your luck.

Scene Four: Thursday

The toilets – boys on stage left, girls on stage right. The Commentators roll two rolls of toilet paper over the floor to each other.

COMMENTATOR 1 Thursday afternoon.

COMMENTATOR 2 The toilets. Boys on the left. Girls on the right.

COMMENTATOR 1 Two stinking, dripping, echoing, monstrous caves tucked away behind the crumbling sports hall.

COMMENTATOR 2 A haven.

COMMENTATOR 1 A hell.

COMMENTATOR 2 A place, at least, where you can talk and teachers won't hear. They don't dare come in here.

COMMENTATOR 1 It's the smell.

COMMENTATOR 2 It's striving to maintain a state of blissful ignorance as to what's really going on ...

In the boys' toilets – Rob and Andrew are at the urinal, Ben is in a cubicle. Dan comes in.

ANDREW   All right?

DAN   Knob off.

ANDREW   Just let it go already. So I dissed your precious girlfriend. So what?

Dan gets out a marker pen. Ben comes out of the cubicle.

BEN   What are you doing?

DAN   Nothing you'd be interested in. Having fun in there, were you?

BEN   Is that the best you can come up with?

Dan writes on one of the walls.

ROB   'For a good time call ...'

BEN   You idiot. You can't do that.

In the girls' toilets – Suze and Izz are at the sinks. Elly is in a cubicle.

SUZE   Elly? Are you OK?

ELLY   Go away.

IZZ   What's wrong? Elly, what's wrong? ... Elly?

ELLY   I just ...

IZZ   We're here for you.

ELLY   Really?

SUZE   Just tell us what's going on.

ELLY   Why? So you can tell everyone else?

DAN   Who's going to stop me? ... She's asking for it anyway. Slapper.

BEN   Has Amy put you up to this?

DAN   Just thought I'd add to the fun.

BEN   This is not fun. This is dangerous, Dan.

DAN   It's none of your business ... It's just a bit of fun ... Are you coming Andy?

Dan and Andrew leave.

BEN   Here. Rob. Give us a hand.

Ben and Rob try to wash it off.

ROB   It won't come off.

BEN   She'll have to change her number.

SUZE   Look. We're your friends. You can talk to us.

ELLY   It's the texts. *(Pause)* I'm really scared.

Elly's phone rings.

SUZE   Are you going to answer it?

ELLY   I'm going to be sick.

SUZE   I'll get it. *(She answers Elly's phone and listens)* Get lost pervert. *(She slams the phone off and thrusts it back to Elly)*

ROB   Whatever. Come on. We'll be late for English.

Rob leaves. Ben remains ... trying to wash it off.

Ben stops. Defeated.

ELLY   They're texting me all the time. And phoning. And emailing. And messaging. And tweeting. They don't leave me alone. Every time I turn on my phone, they're there. Beep beep and my stomach hits the floor. I can't check my computer anymore without feeling sick. I was up all last night ... watching all this hate just ... downloading ... One o' clock in the morning. Beep. Two o' clock. Beep. Three o' clock. Beep. Don't they ever go to sleep?

SUZE   Oh Elly.

ELLY   The texts are the worst. At least you can avoid the computer. But I need my phone.

SUZE   I know babe.

ELLY All the messages end with the same three letters. 'L O L'. As though I shouldn't really be upset by it all. As though it's only a joke ... I want to send messages back to all of them saying: 'You might be laughing out loud, but I'm crying inside, I'm screaming inside.' But there's no quick way of saying that, is there? No one's thought up a clever abbreviation for that, have they? There's no text speak for 'I'm going slowly mad.' Is there?

COMMENTATOR 2 There's no escape from the bullies anymore. They follow you home. Inside your computer. Inside your brain. Texting. Tweeting. Messages constantly beeping. All day. All night. No escape.

COMMENTATOR 1 It's enough to make you mad.

COMMENTATOR 2 But if you've got good friends ...

COMMENTATOR 1 Have you got good friends?

Scene Five: Friday

The bus stop outside school. Everyone there, except Elly, Amy and Dan. The Commentators are eating crisps and cake and dropping crumbs on the floor

COMMENTATOR 1 Friday.

COMMENTATOR 2 The end of the day ... The end of the week.

COMMENTATOR 1 At the bus stop – waiting to be taken home again by the same miserable as sin bus driver.

COMMENTATOR 2 Waiting for the weekend to start.

COMMENTATOR 1 Nearly there ... but still waiting.

COMMENTATOR 2 And tired.

COMMENTATOR 1 Everyone tired. Everyone cross.

COMMENTATOR 2 But you got to keep it under wraps.

COMMENTATOR 1 Teachers – just round the corner.

COMMENTATOR 2 Keeping an eye.

COMMENTATOR 1 So we keep it down.

COMMENTATOR 2 For now ...

Suze, Izz, Ben, Andrew, Rob

ANDREW   Where's Dan?

SUZE   Where's Amy?

IZZ   Where's Elly?

SUZE   They weren't in lessons all afternoon.

IZZ   Ben? Where are they?

BEN   How should I know?

IZZ   Come on, you're the one that's been going on and on about sorting it out.

Everyone looks at Ben. Waiting.

BEN   I ... I spoke to Mrs Johnson.

ROB   The head of year! Why?

BEN   Someone had to. It was out of control. Yesterday, someone sent Elly a death threat.

IZZ   You what?

BEN   I saw her, yesterday afternoon, coming out the toilets, she'd been sick and she was shaking and she looked awful. I asked her about it. She told me. She showed me the messages. Someone had threatened to kill her ... and worse. People all over the internet – threatening her, telling her to kill herself. Awful stuff. Just. Haters. Everywhere. Horrible. I couldn't let that go. I just couldn't. It was going too far.

ANDREW   It was just a bit of fun. It didn't mean anything.

SUZE   Everyone knows that people write a load of rubbish on the internet.

ROB   And texts are just stupid. She should have deleted them and not got herself in such a sweat.

IZZ   Death threats?

BEN   And worse.

IZZ   God.

Dan comes in.

ANDREW   Dan? What's happened?

DAN   Amy's suspended. So am I ... They called the police in.

ROB   The police?

DAN   She's kept them all. Every single message. All of them ... They're all evidence. There's hundreds. Thousands maybe.

ANDREW   Why get the police in though? It was just a bit of a laugh.

DAN   They're saying it's illegal ... harassment. Every person that sent her a text is in trouble ... And they're tracing all the emails and the posts on Amy's video. Me and Amy ...

ROB   You're having a laugh. It's not illegal. How could it be? That's just ...

DAN   It is.

ROB   Shit.

SUZE   Rob? You didn't? Tell me you didn't.

ROB   It was just a bit of fun. Everyone was doing it.

DAN   No one told us it was illegal ... Everyone was doing it.

IZZ   We should have done something – stopped it, spoken to someone.

BEN   Yeah. We should ...

DAN   You'd better watch your back you/

BEN   Look mate. You're in enough trouble already. Don't make it worse.

ANDREW   Leave it, Dan.

ROB   Yeah. Leave it.

DAN   I wouldn't want to share a bus with any of you anyway. I'm walking ...

He leaves.

SUZE   So what happens now?

Elly comes in.

BEN   Elly?

ELLY   Ben ... Thank you.

BEN   What about Amy?

ELLY   Your parents have taken her home.

BEN   And the police?

ELLY   My ... my mum and dad are ... I should've told them last weekend. It's so much worse now.

BEN   It's OK. It's over now. It's sorted.

ELLY   Is it? It's out there now – on the internet – copied, reposted, cached. It's out there forever now. I'm always going to be 'that girl' – college, uni, job interviews. This is never going to go away.

ROB   Elly. I'm so ...

ELLY   Did you mean it Rob? What you said? In that text. Was it true?

ROB   No. God no. I was just a bit mad. It was just ... everyone was ... I'm ... I don't know what to say. I didn't realise ...

ELLY   The police'll be round at yours. They're taking it all so seriously ... I'm sorry.

IZZ   What the hell are you apologising to him for?

Rob goes towards Suze.

SUZE   Get lost Rob.

ROB   I ...

BEN   How could you ...?

COMMENTATOR 1 And so our bus queue is torn apart.

COMMENTATOR 2 We know that a fraction of the blame lies with each of us.

COMMENTATOR 1 For going with the crowd.

COMMENTATOR 2 For being cowardly.

COMMENTATOR 1 For not speaking soon enough.

COMMENTATOR 2 For sending that tweet. For posting that message.

COMMENTATOR 1 For being a hater and thinking it was just a bit of fun.

COMMENTATOR 2 But if you'd been there?

COMMENTATOR 1 What would you have done?

Lights down.

The end.

THREE SHOES

Inspired by the work of eleven Surrey-based youth theatres at the *Celebrate! Festival,* The Harlequin, Redhill, 2009.

Characters: *(Cast may double roles.)*

Eddie
Bishop
Katherine (Eddie's sister)
Mother (Eddie's)
Boy
Harry and Harry (Henry VIII's soldiers)
Artist (1st scene)
Choir boys, servants, town's people, children
Dora
Tom (Dora's older brother)
Girl
Girl 2
Vera (a child star)
Vera's Mother
Stage Manager
Octavia (a social reformer)
Artist (2nd scene)
Zsofia
Phoenix
Reporter
Cameraman
Publicist
Gary and Barry (bodyguards)
Caricaturist
Fans, Paparazzi, Umbrella carrier
Note: A '/' indicates an interruption.

Prologue

Three shoes are abandoned: a patched soft brown leather shoe, a white ballet shoe, and a sparkly stiletto.

Three children run/hobble to their shoes and hurry to put them on – there is a feeling that each one is late.

A boy runs to the leather shoe. He is wearing rags that would not have looked out of place any time from the 1200s to the 1600s. This is Eddie.

A girl runs to the ballet shoe. She is wearing a shabby pink cotton dress in a late 19th century style. This is Dora.

Another girl runs to the stiletto. She is looking uncomfortable in a modern evening dress. This is Zsofia.

The two girls run off. Eddie is left struggling with the laces.

Scene One: Boy Bishop

The square outside a cathedral. Eddie is struggling with his shoe. The Bishop, a youngish man, with the worries of the world on his shoulders, comes up behind him.

BISHOP   You should have been dressed this last half hour.

EDDIE   The other boys threw my shoes out. I couldn't find them.

BISHOP   They will be beaten for it later.

EDDIE   Please don't, Father.

BISHOP   Are you prepared for the sermon?

EDDIE   I think so.

BISHOP   And we won't have any of the jokes we had last year?

EDDIE   No, Father.

BISHOP   I chose you because you are a good boy ... not like the other boys ... I'm trusting you.

EDDIE   Yes, Father.

BISHOP   This is an important day for us.

The Bishop seems lost in thought. Eddie is uncomfortable, uncertain whether he can go or not. Katherine runs up.

KATHERINE   Oh Eddie. You're still here.

EDDIE   What is it?

KATHERINE   Mother wanted me to give you this.

She hands him a package. He opens it. A pearl.

EDDIE   Dad's pearl ... Why?

KATHERINE   She's proud of you. Wants you to carry it with you ... So it'll be like you're carrying him ... us ... all of us.

EDDIE   Oh.

KATHERINE   And you'll look after it. As it's all we have left of him.

EDDIE   Tell her, thanks.

BISHOP   Will you stop chatting and come and get ready?

EDDIE   Sorry, Father.

BISHOP   And remember, none of the japes that did us no favours last year. The King –

KATHERINE   He wouldn't. Eddie's a good boy.

BISHOP   Yes. Well. Hurry up young bishop. Your duties await. Sooner this day is over with, the better. The wind is changing.

Bishop wanders off.

KATHERINE   You aren't planning anything, are you, Eddie?

Eddie looks uncomfortable.

KATHERINE   Eddie?

EDDIE   The other boys ...

KATHERINE   Will lead you wrong. You're doing a good thing for our family, Eddie. Mother is so proud her eyes are shining like a full moon on an autumn night. It's the first time she's looked happy since Father was lost at sea.

EDDIE   But it's the tradition. Every year. The Bishop knows. He likes it. Last year when Charlie lifted up his robe and farted he laughed and laughed and laughed.

KATHERINE   But it's different now ... Can't you see how worried he looks?

EDDIE   I hadn't really/

KATHERINE   And the news of the King's soldiers turned against the Church. And fights in the monasteries, and talk of burning bishops who don't agree with the King wanting to divorce the Queen ...

EDDIE   But we'll be alright.

KATHERINE   The King hates this festival – the Feast of Fools. He hates it that a child is dressed up as a bishop because it is always so rude; it represents everything he hates ... Please Eddie, be sensible. This is a day to bring honour to our family. Not shame.

EDDIE   Alright. Alright Katherine.

KATHERINE   Good. And carry Dad's pearl with you in the procession ... Remember ...

She hangs it in the pouch around his neck.

EDDIE   I will.

KATHERINE   And don't listen to the other boys.

EDDIE   I won't.

KATHERINE   And hurry up ... You should get ready.

EDDIE   Well, if you stopped nagging me ...

Katherine pushes him. He runs off to get ready. She looks nervously at the sky. The artist shambles in, a young man, dressed in clothes that were once smart. He sits in a corner and begins to sketch.

The square comes to life. Garlands are unfurled, a band of musicians sets up, salesmen enter, children dart about, playing. Katherine is joined by her Mother, a couple of soldiers rest in a corner (fairly inconspicuously), townspeople mill about. Perhaps a troupe of travelling performers do some tumbling. A game of dice is played in one corner. There is a general atmosphere of life and colour, of festival celebration.

Then the choir boys process, seemingly demure and soberly dressed. On a signal from one they all turn away and when they turn back they are wearing grotesque gargoyle-like masks, strangely menacing.

The crowd quiets.

EDDIE   Almighty God, by whose grace alone we are accepted and called to Thy service: strengthen us by thy Holy Spirit and make us worthy of our calling.

CHOIR BOYS   Hee Haw.

They bray like donkeys. The bishop tries to quieten them. The crowd laughs. The soldiers are alert.

EDDIE   The Lord strengthens you to serve him all the days of your life.

CHOIR BOYS   Hee Haw.

The boys are louder, and so all the reactions are amplified. One of the soldiers puts a hand on his sword, ready.

Once the crowd has quietened everyone looks at Eddie. He is exceedingly nervous. There is an uncomfortable silence.

BISHOP   Go on.

BOYS   Go on.

CROWD   Go on.

KATHERINE   Be good Eddie. Bring us honour, not shame.

BOYS   Lift up your robe and show us your bum.

MOTHER   Have courage son.

CROWD   Tell us a joke.

BISHOP   Speak the word of our Lord.

CROWD   Start the Feast of Fools with a fart.

BOYS   Do what we told you. Bark like a dog, neigh like a horse, bray like a donkey, squeak like a pig.

KATHERINE   Eddie. Think of our father. Are you carrying his pearl? His only gift to us?

Eddie clasps the pearl. He is frozen, unable to decide. The crowd calls, whistles, and shouts. The choir boys are wild.

Everything carries on but it is as though the sound has been turned down. Another, bigger boy comes up to him.

BOY   You should never have been chosen. What a measly baby you are, Eddie. I'll show you how 'tis done.

The boy goes to pull up Eddie's robe.

EDDIE   No ... I want to do it right ... no fooling. That's why I was chosen. To be Bishop for the day. To do it properly. Holy.

BOY   Holy? Hah! This is properly ... Look at them all. Half-crazed with drink and revelry already ... Give them what they want. A flash of your bum and a bawdy song and a start to the festival.

EDDIE   But the Bishop, the King, my Sister, my Mother. They ...

BOY   Who cares what they want? It's the Feast of Fools ... This is about us for once. One day a year when it's about us who no one ever listens to. This is a day for having a bit of fun without being whipped for it ... And if you don't do it ... (*He strikes his fist into his palm.*)

EDDIE   But honour ...

Boy strikes his fist into his palm again.

Eddie, scared, makes a decision. The world bursts into life again around him. Eddie raises a hand as though in benediction. Everyone quietens. The soldiers edge closer.

EDDIE   Oink. Oink. Oink.

He is about to lift up his robe when the soldiers leap on him.

SOLDIERS   That's enough of that. King's orders.

BISHOP   You promised me, Eddie.

One soldier leaps at the bishop and knocks him out. The choir boys scatter and the crowd, frightened, shrink to the edges of the square.

MOTHER   Leave him. He's just a little boy. Please. In the name of Our Lord God. Leave him.

SOLDIER   Get away. It's ... what's that word Harry?

SOLDIER 2   Sacrilegious, Harry.

SOLDIER   Yeah ... We've got our orders. Sacrilegious activities forbidden. Constitutes high treason. Punishable by death.

EDDIE   I just did what the other boys told me to do.

SOLDIER 2   A likely story. You'll answer to Lord Cromwell.

MOTHER   Please. Have mercy.

KATHERINE   He's just a stupid child.

SOLDIER   Out of our way.

MOTHER   You shall not take him ... He's a child. He's my child.

SOLDIER 2   A child dressed in the robes of a Bishop. It ain't right.

KATHERINE   It's an old tradition.

SOLDIER 2   No room for old traditions nowadays. Out of my way or I'll strike you down.

SOLDIER   Steady, Harry.

SOLDIER 2   I'm your superior, Harry, and you'll follow my orders or else ... (*He strikes his fist into his palm.*)

EDDIE   Please. Let me go. I wasn't going to do it ... Just with the crowd shouting and the other boys and ...

He starts to cry. The soldiers confer, over his head.

SOLDIER   Harry? What do we do?

SOLDIER 2   We take him in, Harry.

SOLDIER   There'll be an uproar. Look at him, he's a snivelling lad. He's just a kid.

SOLDIER 2   We'll leave him.

SOLDIER   Our orders?

SOLDIER 2   We'll say he escaped ... We'll say he kicked you on the shin and he escaped into the crowd and we couldn't find him again.

SOLDIER   Good.

Soldier lets Eddie go. Soldier 2 kicks Soldier hard on the shin.

SOLDIER   What did you do that for?

SOLDIER 2   So you'll have a bruise ... evidence.

SOLDIER   He doesn't have feet the size of your great clodhoppers.

SOLDIER 2   Sorry, Harry.

SOLDIER   All this fuss over a kid.

The soldiers go, leaving Eddie on the floor. Everyone else starts to leave.

KATHERINE   Come Mother, leave him.

She leads her Mother away ... they barely look at Eddie.

EDDIE   I didn't mean it. It was the other boys. They made me. It's what we always do. I'm sorry ... I never wanted to be up there anyway. (*Desperately*) I didn't ask to be put up there.

Suddenly everyone has gone apart from the unconscious Bishop, the artist and Eddie.

The artist continues to draw.

EDDIE   Why are you still drawing? ... There's nothing here worth remembering. Stop it. Stop drawing me. Stop it.

The artist continues to draw. Thunder rumbles in the distance.

Entr'acte 1

Note: Text can be spoken by individual cast members, some or all. Company may interpret as they wish.

CAST

A cry rose up and shook the theatre,

A hundred people watched,

No one blinked.

The cry got louder, the theatre quaked,

A thousand people listened,

No one got out of their seat.

The cry became a scream, the theatre started to break,

A million people saw and heard,

No one tried to comfort her.

And so she cried for the longest time,

She cried for hours, days, months, years, decades, centuries,

She cried for eternity,

Waiting for someone to reach out a hand,

Waiting for someone to hear her,

And, more than anything,

It felt like hunger.

Scene Two: All That Glitters

The street outside a rehearsal room. A few children are gathering by a sign that says, 'Auditions Today .' They are mostly wearing ragged dresses and most have bare feet.

The stage manager, not much older than the children, but full of importance, comes out into the street and starts looking at the children, some of whom show off for his benefit.

Dora arrives, dressed even worse than the others, dragged by her brother.

TOM   Will you stop struggling you little wretch? You want to be here if you don't want a thrashing ... You're a fine dancer and the family has to eat ... Mother's sick and Father, well ...

Dora looks like she's about to answer.

TOM   No lip little sister. Dance your best. Get a part and it's three shillings a week. You'll be a fairy or a angel or, I dunno, a little bird or something ... And you'll 'ave white satin ballet shoes and wear a pretty dress ... all red velvet and silver stars ... and flowers in yer hair. You'll love it. And it'll put food on the table for all of us ... You're better than the rest of this lot put together. Ain't I taught you how to tumble?

DORA   Yes, Tom.

TOM   Start stretching ... They'll be calling people soon. I'll have a word to the stage manager. Fuss 'n I'll clout you.

Tom wanders over to the stage manager.

An artist arrives and starts sketching the scene. The girls pose for him. He shows little interest in them individually and they start looking for something else to do. They notice Dora who is warming up.

GIRL   Who's this?

GIRL 2   New face.

GIRL   She ain't got a chance.

GIRL 2   Pathetic.

GIRL   Look at her. Limbering up. Who does she think she is? Ruddy street tumbler. Better class of performer needed here.

GIRL 2   Indeed.

GIRL   None of them 'penny in me 'at' girls wanted here. I was an angel in *Babes in the Wood* last Christmas. You need to be refined for this lark.

GIRL 2   And we was fairy folk year before that in *Mother Goose* ... Proper beautiful we was.

GIRL   Don't even look like she wants to be 'ere.

GIRL 2   Which of us does?

GIRL   The money's good.

GIRL 2   Good enough to put up with the bleeding feet?

GIRL   Breaking backs?

GIRL 2   Staring old men?

GIRL   Never enough money for that ... Not when they come round the dressing rooms ...

GIRL 2   Or wait at the stage doors.

GIRL   Holding their umbrellas. Looking so – hungry.

GIRL 2   No glamour in this world ... Someone should tell her.

They debate. Vera arrives with her mother – a real contrast to the other girls – in expensive, well-made clothes. Vera wears a pearl necklace.

VERA   This is a disgrace, using the artists' entrance with the chorus. Don't they know who I am?

MOTHER   Yes dear. But they did explain/

VERA   I don't care for the reason. I want a little respect. I am, after all, the star of the show. People pay to see me, not these ragamuffins.

MOTHER   Yes dear, but the other children in the show make you look so darling and sweet ...

VERA   Ugh, look at them all – staring at me.

MOTHER   Be pleasant, dear.

VERA   Hello. Hello. Yes. That's right. It's me. Vera, the child star, the infant prodigy. 'An adorable angel' said the *Times*. 'A picture of natural innocence' said the *Sunday Pictorial*. 'A blessing to London' said the *Herald*. 'A treasure' said ... said ...

GIRL *(under her breath)* What is she? An actress or a walking, talking newspaper?

VERA   Why is this taking so long? Why is the door closed? Mother. Go and find out what's going on.

Her Mother goes. She is left alone.

Some of the girls are genuinely excited to see such a star. They crowd round her.

VERA   Don't push. Don't crowd me. Don't touch me with your grubby hands, you urchins.

They start jostling her. Partly out of excitement and partly out of mischief. Her necklace breaks – pearls roll everywhere.

VERA   My necklace! Oh help. My necklace.

The girls run after the pearls.

VERA   Give them back. Give them back to me. You horrid girls. Give them back at once.

GIRL   Fight us for them.

VERA   I certainly will not fight you ... Help! Help! Thievery! Treachery!

GIRL 2   No one will help you. This pearl will feed my family for a month. You should be glad to give it.

The girls huddle away from Vera, revelling. Vera starts to cry.

VERA   You wicked girls. That necklace was a family heirloom – it brings me luck.

One pearl has been picked up by Dora. She brings it over.

DORA   They won't bring 'em back. 'n if you call for Peelers they'll scarper before 'e's a street away ... 'ere though. I think this un's the biggest.

VERA   Thank you ... What's your name?

DORA   Dora.

VERA   Dora ... Keep it ... One pearl is no good to me without the others. It's ruined now. You have it. Perhaps it will bring you luck.

DORA   I ain't never seen nothing so beautiful.

A moment of embarrassment.

VERA   Well, I really don't know what's keeping them. This is absurd. I'm the star of this show – 'A thing of pure beauty' said the director. 'A blessed lamb' said the stage manager.

GIRL   'A bloomin' nuisance' said everyone else.

VERA   I will see to it that you are not given a part. You are too ugly to play a toad. And you are a thief.

She goes.

Thunder rumbles overhead.

The girls all start moaning and complaining to the Stage Manager.

STAGE MANAGER Listen. You don't get let in til eleven to see the Producer. Those are theatre rules and those are my rules and those are rules we'll stick by. A little rain won't hurt you.

Octavia enters. She is young, softly spoken with a steely determination. She carries a bright red parasol.

OCTAVIA   They will catch colds and pneumonias and add to the great plague of disease in the filthy dwellings they go home to and you shall be held responsible. And then where will your chorus of stars and fairies be? Shivering with fever and dead of cholera with their brothers and sisters.

STAGE MANAGER I'll thank you not to interfere, Ma'am.

OCTAVIA   I have a right to be here. To help these poor children.

GIRL   We don't want your help.

GIRL 2   Your help don't bring no three shillins a week home to my family.

OCTAVIA   Your precious childhood should not be spent grubbing around in these sinful places ... I am taking a group of children to the countryside for some fresh air and clean living. Will some of you choose to join me? ... Any of you?

GIRL   Not me.

GIRL 2   Come on. Let us in. I don't mind a bit of thunder, but I can't stomach listening to her preaching.

STAGE MANAGER Not til it's eleven.

GIRL   Well, how long til then?

STAGE MANAGER About half a minute ... So you'd best get yourselves ready. You look more like a chorus of goblins than fairies.

They start getting ready in earnest. Octavia watches. She approaches Dora.

OCTAVIA   I've not seen you around here before, child.

DORA   No, Miss.

OCTAVIA   What's your name?

DORA   Dora, Miss.

OCTAVIA   Wouldn't you rather come with me, Dora? A lovely stay in the countryside and then we will teach you to read and write. And you shall have a clean new dress. What do you say?

Dora thinks.

DORA   Will it be red velvet?

OCTAVIA   Will what be red velvet?

DORA   The new dress.

OCTAVIA   Heavens, no. It will be pink cotton gingham, like the other girls.

DORA   Oh.

OCTAVIA   Red velvet indeed. What an idea.

Tom comes over.

TOM   You ready?

OCTAVIA   Are you responsible for this child?

TOM   She's my sister, Ma'am.

OCTAVIA   You will be pleased to hear that I am offering her an opportunity to better herself.

TOM   Pleased nothing. She'll get a job in the panto and help feed her family.

OCTAVIA   Wouldn't you rather she had clean air and a chance to learn to read and write?

TOM   And let her family starve to death? We all do our bit, lady. Her brother's a sweep. Her sister sells pins and matches ... And Dora here ... well, she got bones like rubber and can turn herself inside out and jump like she's made from air – and earn good money at it.

OCTAVIA   So you sell your siblings into slavery. Does that make you proud?

TOM   It keeps us alive.

OCTAVIA   And what do you want, Dora?

Tom takes Dora by the arm and almost drags her towards the door.

TOM   You must sing as well as dance ... but I told him you sing like a bird. Which you will do or – *(Thumps his fist into his hand.)*

Dora looks back at Octavia.

TOM   All this fuss over a kid.

The other girls crowd in after them.

We see, momentarily, into the audition room. Dora is standing alone, watched by everyone. She sings something sweet and charming and then dances. She really is talented. And, just for a moment, she seems alive.

Tom and the stage manager discuss terms.

Dora suddenly stumbles in her dance, and the other girls lean in greedily.

The artist continues drawing.

Thunder rumbles closer and a first few spots of rain start to fall.

Entr'acte 2

CAST *(as previously)*

Those accidental accidents

The moments where nothing goes precisely to plan

The instant you weren't expecting

When it all just falls apart

And everyone's watching.

The moment when you miss your cue

When the gun shot comes after you've already pulled the trigger, screamed, and died

When the telephone rings after you've already picked it up and said hello

When you wait for a line that never comes

When you fall

When you fail

When the music is too loud

When the music is too quiet

When the lights don't change

When the lights do change

When you lose your shoe

When you realise a prop has been forgotten

When the audience doesn't get it

When they *do*

Those accidental accidents

What do you do then?

Do you wait in miserable, uncomfortable, unbending silence, broken by those watchers in the dark

Shifting in their seats?

Do you wait, uncertain?

Or do you stand there – proud, sure, ready, alert – looking for the moment when, unnoticed, you can

Pick yourself up

And shine?

Because this is your moment in the spotlight

And no one's going to take it from you

Not until you're ready.

Scene Three: Close Up

A red carpet is unrolled.

Fans are gathering by the barriers.

A cheap caricaturist is wandering about trying to cadge a sale off anyone. No one is interested. He doesn't give up though and approaches everyone asking if he can sketch them, showing his sample book of celebrities with overlarge heads.

A tired reporter is about to record a piece to camera.

REPORTER   Come on, let's get it over with.

CAMERAMAN What's your problem Janey?

REPORTER I hate these red carpet premieres. So boring. Stupid screaming fans ... Stars I've never even heard of ... And it's raining. I hate it. Hate it.

CAMERAMAN This is Showbiz Janey. Showbiz with a capital SHOW.

REPORTER Well, I'm fed up with it.

CAMERAMAN Ready to do your piece to camera?

REPORTER Quicker the better.

CAMERAMAN Focus Janey. And ... Recording ... five, four, three, two, one ...

REPORTER (*lots of very fake energy*) Hello and welcome to the Leicester Square Red Carpet Television Channel and to tonight's premiere of the new film that EVERYONE is talking about. We'll be bringing you all the action from the carpet. Meeting the fans. Meeting the celebs. And most importantly meeting the stars of the film – hot and fabulous young actors – Zsofia and Phoenix. (*Beat*) While we're waiting for them to arrive, let's go and meet some of the fans.

She goes over to the people gathering at the barriers. As soon as they see the camera they start screaming.

REPORTER Wow! I can hardly hear myself! Let's talk to some of these crazy people. Hi. Hello. What's your name?

FAN I'm Ceri.

REPORTER Tell me Ceri – how long have you been waiting here?

FAN Me and my friends have, like, been here for, like, seven hours.

REPORTER It's freezing here. How've you coped with the rain and the cold?

FAN We don't care about the rain.

REPORTER   And tell me, who are you most excited about seeing?

FAN   Phoenix. Oh my god. He's so gorgeous.

Her friends all scream 'Phoenix, Phoenix' ...

REPORTER (*hopelessly*) And have you read the book the film is based on?

FAN   I just, like, love Phoenix so much. And, like, Zsofia is so amazing and so beautiful ... And we're so jealous of her, like, getting to work with Phoenix, like, every day.

REPORTER   There we go. Thank you girls. I hope you get to see the stars. Let's talk to another fan ... Hello. What's your name?

FAN 2   I'm Alistair. Hi.

REPORTER   And what excites you about this film.

FAN 2   Zsofia innit. She's gorgeous.

REPORTER   Yes. Thank you. (*Signals to the cameraman to stop recording.*) I wanted to make hard-hitting award winning documentaries about political intrigue.

CAMERAMAN Yeah, and I wanted to make James Bond movies. Come on. Those kids will be arriving soon.

The two stars arrive with their retinue. They are both young but stylishly dressed in black with touches of red satin and velvet. A publicist hovers behind them, along with bodyguards. Two umbrella holders try to keep them covered with bright red golfing umbrellas (though their job is not made easy by the stars who seem oblivious to their presence.)

The fans go crazy.

The stars go over to them and start signing autographs / posing with them for photos, etc.

One fan, particularly crazed, breaks away from the barriers and rushes towards the stars. The two bodyguards immediately step in front of them.

We suddenly become aware of the caricaturist again. He starts sketching the scene furiously, getting as close as he can to the action.

GARY   Oh no you don't, sunshine.

BARRY   None of that, thank you.

GARY   That's not the way we like our premieres. Is it, Barry?

BARRY   Not at all, Gary. Not at all.

CRAZY FAN   I just want to touch them.

GARY   Well, I can guarantee they don't want to touch you, and that's the truth.

BARRY   God's truth.

CRAZY FAN   Phoenix. Zsofia. I just want to touch you.

BARRY   Now. Now. Move along now.

GARY   I think we might have to do a bit of helping, Barry.

BARRY   I think you're right, Gary.

GARY   Do I need to call Harry?

BARRY   I think we can manage this one. It's only small.

The fan sobs.

GARY   And overcome with emotion I'd say, wouldn't you?

BARRY   Overcome. Absolutely.

GARY   All this fuss over a pair of kids.

They gently pick up the fan and place him/her out of the way.

They shove the caricaturist. He makes his way towards the reporter and starts making sketches of the two child stars.

The stars, meanwhile, make their way over to the bank of photographers and pose for photographs. Although they start off fairly decorously, after a while their poses become lewd and provocative. The publicist steps in and moves them on.

REPORTER   Zsofia ... Phoenix. Over here ...

The publicist nods and they go over.

REPORTER   Just a couple of questions.

ZSOFIA   Hi.

REPORTER   Zsofia, you look wonderful. Tell us about what you're wearing.

ZSOFIA   It's a special *Gucci* creation, designed specially for me. I just love it.

REPORTER   And what about in your hair? Is that stunning jewellery also *Gucci?*

ZSOFIA   No. That's mine. It was my great-great-grandmother's pearl, given to her by a famous actress, like, two hundred years ago or something. It's sort of my lucky charm.

REPORTER   Brilliant. Lovely to see some vintage accessorising going on.

ZSOFIA   It's a bit more important than that/

REPORTER   So ... Did you enjoy making the film?

ZSOFIA   Oh yes. It was a wonderful experience. I loved it.

REPORTER   What was the best thing?

ZSOFIA   Oh definitely working with the director, Sam ... He's an absolute genius.

REPORTER   How about you, Phoenix?

PHOENIX   I loved all of it. The whole thing.

REPORTER   This is your fourth film together now. You've been a very successful acting partnership ... Are you planning on a fifth film together?

Both hesitate. The publicist jumps in.

PUBLICIST   Although there are no immediate plans for a fifth film – Zsofia and Phoenix are hoping to continue working together.

There is a sudden change in the atmosphere.

REPORTER   There have been lots of rumours in the press lately about Phoenix spending some time in rehab ... What do you have to say about that, Phoenix?

Phoenix is about to answer ...

PUBLICIST   It's a story invented by cheap journalists. Phoenix has been working very hard lately and took some time out to rest at a beach resort ... Any other story is nonsense.

REPORTER   And how about the alleged nude photographs taken of you Zsofia? ... How do you justify that, with your celebrated 'Girl Next Door' image?

Zsofia is about to answer.

PUBLICIST   Zsofia never posed for those photographs. It was a very clever bit of photoshopping ... Now if you will excuse us ... Come on.

The publicist sweeps them away, knocking into the caricaturist on her way. The reporter loses her temper.

REPORTER   And how about the online gambling, Phoenix? ... And how about the bottles of alcohol found in your trailer, Zsofia? ... And how about the fact that you're both frauds. You play beautiful innocent children but you're about as innocent as snakes. Our viewers want to know the truth about you. Our viewers want to know the truth.

CAMERAMAN What was that about?

REPORTER   Bit of investigative journalism.

CAMERAMAN Get a grip. Come on ... you're burnt out. Let's get a coffee.

They leave.

PUBLICIST   What online gambling? ... No. Don't tell me now. Tell me later. I can't believe you two. The rain's getting worse. Come on. Inside now.

PHOENIX   I want to sign more autographs.

ZSOFIA   I want to pose for more photographs.

PUBLICIST   Inside now. Do as I say.

ZSOFIA   No.

PUBLICIST   Don't argue with me. Your contract ...

ZSOFIA   Screw the contract.

PHOENIX   Tear it up.

PUBLICIST   You're only famous because of me. You are little plastic dolls and notebooks and computer games and ready meals because of me. I'd tread carefully if I was you. And get inside the cinema right now.

A moment of utter defiance.

ZSOFIA   No.

PHOENIX   No.

At that moment the storm breaks properly. Thunder and lightning and rain.

Someone bumps into the caricaturist sending his sketchbook flying.

After a flash of lightning the lights go out. There are cries of 'torches, torches' and when a few torches are lit the stage is bare apart from Zsofia and Phoenix who have been joined by (or have become) Eddie and Dora.

Epilogue

CAST *(as previously)*

You will not tell us what to do.

You will not dress us up like dolls.

All these years of being looked at and never listened to.

All these years of being adored and never loved.

We are on your stages,

On your screens,

Faces big as houses.

We are perfect.

We are silent.

We are freckle-faced, smooth-skinned, smiling, grinning, laughing on cue, children of nature.

We are funny.

We are tragic.

We are whatever you want us to be.

We speak your words, the words that have been written for us.

We dance your dances and wear your clothes.

You destroy us.

With your money and your drugs and your booze and your gossip and your love.

You destroy us completely.

And then, when we are destroyed – you hate us.

This hurts.

Your desire for us to be so effortlessly talented.

Your desire to model us out of plastic and sell us for £9.99.

Your desire for us ...

And all the time our feet are bleeding,

and our faces sore from smiling.

So, enough.

No more bishops

Or brothers

Or publicists.

Now it's our time to have a voice

Now it's our time for you to listen.

Just us.

Children with something to say about their future, about their world, about what they believe in,

About what they see ...

Too many years of silence.

Here we are ...

Here we are ...

They are ready to speak.

[Note: Each company can add their own words here: What do the young performers want to say? What do they believe in? What do they see? This is their chance to be heard – everyone is listening to them.]

The pictures which were previously drawn or painted by the artists fall like leaves from a tree in Autumn.

The lights go off suddenly. When the lights come on again all that is left are the same three shoes we saw at the beginning, with a red umbrella suspended above them.

Lights down.

The end.

NOAH

For Chichester Festival Youth Theatre, 2012.

Characters:

Noah

Mrs Noah

Ham, Shem, Japeth – Noah's sons

Hanna – Ham's wife

Sarah – Shem's wife

Judith – Japeth's wife

Martin, Sandra: sinners

Etta – a dove

Elephant, Wolf, Tiger, Mouse

Many Other Animals

Note: A '/' indicates an interruption.

Scene One

As we walk into the ark we see rejected signs, 'God's Boat', 'Family Ship', 'Big Yacht', etc.

A chorus of animals are watching. Occasionally, we catch a glimpse of one of them.

On the ark.

Noah is measuring a plank of wood. He measures it over and over again, viewing it from different angles – measuring every dimension possible. At one point he goes to saw it, pauses and begins measuring again. After measuring again he thinks about sawing it but rubs it down with sandpaper instead.

Occasionally, throughout this activity, one of his sons or their wives wanders past and watches him for a moment or two.

Noah abandons the plank of wood and appears to be listening to the heavens, nodding and writing down a list in a small notebook with a tiny stub of pencil. He finishes listening and looks back over his notes.

NOAH   Are you there Lord? ... It's just ... only one thing ... are you sure about the snakes? ... I'm not questioning you as such it's just ... well ... you know ... and don't get cross ... but you don't have such a good track record with snakes, what with the garden, the apple ... all that ... messy business ... and no-one would blame you if ... well ... I'm just saying ... it's going to be a bit of a squeeze anyway ... and no questions would be asked, *(Beat)* seeing as how there'll be no-one to ask the questions ... And ... well, snakes *(Beat)* on a boat ... sounds like a recipe for disaster. Don't you think? *(Gets a paper cut from his notebook)* You could just say 'No.' Yes, I think I've got it all ... *(Listens)* No, no, complete sense ... Not a cloud of doubt in my mind, or the sky for that matter *(Hesitates)* ... I'm building you a boat, a very very large boat *(Listens)* ... yes, the biggest boat ever to have been built since the dawn of time ...

I'm filling it with two of every kind of animal, seven of the clean ones, and enough food and bedding to last a year. I'm putting my family on the boat. You're sending a flood. Every human and beast other than those on my ... your ... our ... boat is going to drown. Crystal clear. *(A moment)* Are you still there? ... It's just ... I was wondering – should I be building a rudder – a rudder – you know, for steering? ... Steering, setting the boat on a particular course towards ... towards a destination? ... Errr ... No? ... Fair enough ... *(Listens)* Tides ... Wind ... Trust ... I do trust you Lord ... Well, I wouldn't be building this boat if ... Sorry ...

Noah carries on measuring. After much looking to the heavens he takes up the saw and starts to cut the plank of wood. Within a few cuts he realises he's gone wrong.

NOAH   Oh bother.

He gets another plank of wood and starts the process again.

For the last little while, Noah's children have been gathered around watching him.

SARAH   Well, I'm worried about him.

JUDITH   Me too.

HANNAH   I think he's losing it.

SARAH   Shhh.

HAM   It's time we asked the daft old coot what he's doing.

SHEM   He's building something.

HAM   Genius.

SHEM   What more do you need to know? He'll tell us when he's ready.

HAM   It's been months. This thing is massive.

JAPETH   So much wood.

JUDITH   I'm fed up of picking splinters out of you ... His hands are cut to shreds ... Who'd love a carpenter?

SARAH   And you've done your back in. Lugging all those trees.

HAM   It's time he told us.

SHEM   Who are you to give our father orders?

JAPETH   Actually, I'm with Ham on this one Brother ... I love our father, I trust him, but I'm going mad with curiosity ...

JUDITH   Me too.

SHEM   Well, I trust him ...

SARAH   And so do I.

HAM   It's not about trust ... it's about respect.

SHEM   Yes, we respect our father.

HAM   But does he respect us?

JAPETH   Let's not overcomplicate things Ham ... we should stand together ... Brothers?

HAM   Brothers.

SHEM   Brothers.

Noah is talking to God.

NOAH   You know how I feel about my family ... They're everything to me ... I'll do anything to keep them safe. *(Beat)* It's time to tell them isn't it? You're right here with me, aren't you? I don't know how to ... I don't know what words to use. *(Listens)* Oh. Thank you. *(To the boys)* Boys ... Where's your mother? There's something I have to tell you all.

SHEM   You see. I told you he'd tell us when he was ready.

NOAH   I appreciate your trust in me, son.

SHEM   In you and God. I am ready to serve, and so is my Sarah.

Noah and Shem have a moment.

NOAH Will you fetch your mother? Call for her or something.

BOYS Mum! ... Muuuum! ... Muuuuummmmm!

MRS NOAH Grief boys ... Enough shouting ... I'm here.

NOAH Oh ... you're here ... Right ... Girls, boys, my love, I suppose you've been wondering what we've been doing.

HAM Oh no.

HANNAH Not at all.

HAM You know we trust you completely.

NOAH It's been very good of you to put yourselves into a project without really knowing what it was ... You're good children ... All of you. I'm very grateful to the Lord to have such blessed sons and daughters-in-law.

SHEM We do our best.

JUDITH We all love you.

SHEM And respect you.

NOAH I know the last few months have been a struggle ... I appreciate all your hard work.

SHEM It was nothing.

SARAH We're pleased to help you.

A moment.

MRS NOAH What's wrong Noah?

A beat.

NOAH *(to Mrs Noah – faltering)* Will you love me? Whatever happens next, will you love me?

MRS NOAH You're an easy man to love, Noah.

NOAH Right ... So ... This thing we've been building ... Any guesses?

SHEM   A new house?

NOAH   Not exactly.

SARAH   A store room?

NOAH   Of sorts.

JAPETH   A shop?

NOAH   No.

JUDITH   A hospital?

NOAH   Perhaps at times. Hopefully not too often.

Silence.

Hannah raises her arm.

NOAH   Yes, Hannah?

HANNAH *(quietly)* It's a boat.

ALL *(except Noah)* A boat?

HANNAH   Before I married Ham and came to live with you all … here … in this awful wasteland … I lived near the sea … There's something about this thing that reminds me of a boat. A massive, massive boat.

HAM   Well, Father? Is it? Is it a boat?

NOAH   Yes.

MRS NOAH   You'd better explain.

NOAH   Well, God said to me 'build a boat" and gave me the dimensions … so this thing we're standing on – it's a boat.

HAM   There must be more to it than that.

NOAH   Well … there's this flood on the way/

JAPETH   Flood?

NOAH   Yes, the Lord is sending a flood to wipe away all of humanity and he's asked me to gather two of every kind of animal and put them on a boat … That's it really.

HANNAH   That's it?

JUDITH   But why?

NOAH   It's all the sin. I've tried, haven't I? All the preaching. Years of it ... It hasn't worked ... I'm not a very good preacher, it turns out. He *(Looking at the sky)* wants a fresh start.

MRS NOAH   And you're the fresh start?

NOAH   We are.

MRS NOAH   Of course we are. Well ... Well good ... Well done everybody. Now/

SARAH   Just one question ...

SHEM   Shhh Sarah ... we don't need to ask questions.

NOAH   It's alright son, she can ask.

SARAH   Where do we get the animals from? Two of every kind ... Every kind ... That's ... um ... quite ... err ... that's quite a lot of animals to go and find.

NOAH   Have a look out in the field.

They all go to have a look.

JAPETH   Oh boy.

MRS NOAH   That grass will never be the same again.

NOAH   They all turned up this morning ... I've got a list ... From God ... I've been checking them off.

HAM   So many animals.

NOAH   ... And, well, the boat's mostly finished so ...

SHEM   That explains that awful sticky pitch stuff ... Sealant ... This thing's waterproof ... And it will float. Genius, Dad. Absolute genius! And the big hatch ... For the big animals. I see ... I see ... Wow ... I'm very impressed ... Do you see? It all makes sense now. Wow ... It's massive ... And we built it ... We did ... Genius!

HANNAH   We're days from the sea … How are we ever going to get this thing to the water? It's huge.

NOAH   That's the thing with this flood you see … We don't have to get the boat to water, the water's coming to the boat.

HANNAH   In the worst drought ever known, since time began?

NOAH   I know it's a lot to ask of you. Please children, I love you all and want to keep you safe with me. You've just got to trust in God.

MRS NOAH   Right. Girls – you're with me. Back to the house … There's some serious packing to do …

JUDITH   I'll gather herbs – in case anything gets sick.

SARAH   What do those waddley ones eat? … I've never seen them before … And what about those ones with the huge ears? Those ones are massive – they'll eat loads. How are we meant to know what to feed them all?

They leave.

NOAH   Boys, I'd be grateful for your help with loading the animals … Would you mind checking over the list?

The boys go out. Mrs Noah returns.

MRS NOAH   Provisions for how long, my love?

NOAH   About a year, I think. He says/

MRS NOAH   A year … Right.

A moment – Noah looks lost.

MRS NOAH   My sweet Noah. Look at you … Best thing is not to panic. We'll be fine. You trust God. He trusts you. I trust you.

NOAH   It's just … It's all … It's just all so big. I'm not sure … I just … feel … I don't know if I can/

MRS NOAH   Of course you can … You're my Noah.

NOAH   Quite.

MRS NOAH   Provisions ... For a year ... It's a good thing I've been putting some things by ... I knew something was up ... didn't think it was a great big flood though.

NOAH   You're a wonder.

MRS NOAH   Maybe go and have a sit down somewhere quiet for a minute ... It's all going to be OK, so long as we keep the family together.

She leaves.

NOAH *(to himself)* He knows what He's doing, He knows what He's doing ...

He wanders away, taking the plank of wood with him.

The loading of the animals: Shem heaves the elephant onto the boat with much effort; Japeth carefully herds the tiger as though a circus tamer with much fear; Ham walks along with the wolf, almost as though they're friends. Then all three boys chase after a tiny mouse that runs everywhere until they finally catch him.

JAPETH   Right. So. We've nearly got them all on. Just a few stragglers.

SHEM   The boat's bursting at the seams.

HAM   I wish he'd told me it was a boat ... I could have ... I don't know – got some charts or something ... studied the stars or something.

Noah returns.

NOAH   Sons. How are you getting on?

JAPETH   We're done, I think.

NOAH   Good. Good ... I've brought the dovecote from home ... Thought they might like it.

The girls return.

MRS NOAH   Right ... Ham, Japeth ... help the women load in the provisions ... Judith's got enough herbs and lotions and potions and odd smelling things to cure an army for eternity ... And I think we've packed enough food. Sarah's fretting about what they all eat but I've told her they'll eat what we've got or they'll go hungry and that's the best we can do.

HAM   Well, we can always set up a barbecue on deck.

NOAH   No ... No killing things while we're on the water. No meat at all ... or fish for that matter ... God was very specific about that.

Whilst they've been talking Martin has crept up, unnoticed by the humans, although perhaps spotted by the animals.

MARTIN   So, I find you here, do I, Mr Noah?

NOAH   What do you want? ... Get off my boat.

MARTIN   I said to the others in the village. I said to them. It's that Noah – strange old man that he is – this is something to do with him. It's been odd all day – strange animals come walking through the village, animals like we've never seen before. And two of each of 'em. Very odd. And then I said, 'I think it's got something to do with that Noah. Strange old man that he is. Hidden up here not seeing any of us for days, weeks maybe. Not coming down and watching our gambling and tutting and sighing and preaching at us like usual. It's that Noah I said. He's planning something.' And I was right ... What's the plan then Noah?

NOAH *(apologetically)* Well, I'm afraid the Lord God Almighty is sending a terrible flood to cleanse the Earth of all the sinners in it. I'm taking these animals and my family with me on this boat and we will sail into a new pure time, free of sin and wickedness. Really am terribly sorry.

MRS NOAH   So get yourself gone. We don't need any spectators, thank you.

MARTIN   Oh they'll laugh themselves sick at this. Laugh themselves sick. I knew something was up, never thought it was this ... Completely cracked. Ha ha ha.

He leaves.

NOAH *(after him)* You could try repenting ... It might not be too late ... Oh what's the use?

SHEM   It's OK, Dad ... Ignore him ... Ignore all of them ... Don't let them upset you. Everyone's on the boat. All the family. All the animals. Shall we close the door? Shall we ... shall we batten down the hatches?

NOAH   Yes ... Yes ... It's time ... Come on, family. Let's close the doors.

HANNAH   But the sky is clear ... It's boiling hot ... There's not a chance it'll rain.

NOAH   You have to trust the Lord Hannah – it's/

MRS NOAH   Shall we not ask any more questions, children? It's a lovely boat and/

NOAH   Ark.

MRS NOAH   What?

NOAH   He calls it an ark. Actually He calls it my ark.

MRS NOAH   Noah's Ark.

NOAH   If nobody minds ... I quite like it.

MRS NOAH   Of course nobody minds.

NOAH   I made a sign.

He unveils the plank of wood, on which is painted 'NOAH'S ARK .'

MRS NOAH   Well then, all aboard Noah's Ark ... And Sarah – perhaps you'd see about getting the kettle on. I put a box of biscuits at the top of one of the crates.

They shut the doors.

HANNAH   But there's no rain.

HAM   Hush, love.

HANNAH   But/

HAM   I know ... Just ... You know ... Family ... Just ... go
with it.

*They busy themselves – unpacking things, tidying boxes away. Mrs
Noah comes back with mugs of tea. They wait. Martin returns with
Sandra. Occasional sounds of animals nearby; maybe one pops up
every now and then.*

SANDRA   So, you're saying that old Noah's got his family
cooped up in that gigantic wooden thing?

MARTIN   Yep, and a load of animals too.

SANDRA   So he's lost it completely then?

MARTIN   Well, it's a change to him coming round the village
doing his old preaching business.

SANDRA   It's Mrs Noah I feel sorry for ... A nice old woman.

MRS NOAH *(from off)* A little less of the old please ... We can hear
you down here.

SANDRA *(quieter)* I wouldn't have got on the boat in the first place
if it was you and me.

MARTIN   Seven days they've been on that boat ... And it's got
hotter and hotter and hotter.

SANDRA   Not a cloud in the sky.

MARTIN   Driest spell we've ever had.

SANDRA   Hasn't rained for months.

MARTIN   That's what you get for believing in that stupid God
of Noah's.

NOAH *(from off)* Repent ... It's still not too late ... If you wouldn't
mind.

MARTIN   Silly old fool. *(To Noah)* How's it going down there?

NOAH *(from off)* It's very good thank you ... Umbrellas and wellington boots at the ready.

MARTIN   You're mad. Mad Mad Mad Old Man. And your stupid God has forgotten all about you.

SANDRA   Yeah, if there even is a God.

NOAH   Lord ... if you were thinking of sending a sign of any sorts ... Now would be a good time.

A first drop of rain.

SANDRA   Did you just feel something?

MARTIN   No.

A second drop.

SANDRA   That was a bird ... A bird passing overhead ... That's lucky, that is.

NOAH   Thank you Lord – crystal clear.

A third drop.

MARTIN   Another bird ... What are the chances? It's our lucky day. Hey Noah! Fancy a game of cards?

NOAH   I think you'll find it's just started raining.

The rain starts coming down in earnest. Martin and Sandra panic.

SANDRA   He was right. He was right. We're going to drown. We're going to drown.

MARTIN   Hold your nerve, it's just a little cloudburst.

SANDRA   There weren't any clouds five seconds ago.

MARTIN   We'll be fine ... We'll be fine ... There's nothing to worry about.

SANDRA   Noah ... Noah ... Let us on your/

MARTIN   What are you doing?

SANDRA   I don't want to drown ... Noah ... Mr Noah. Please/

MARTIN   It's just a shower ... It's not a flood ... Don't go crawling to that old man – he's just got lucky. Or it's a bit of his magic. There's nothing to worry about; he's just trying to scare us.

SANDRA   Perhaps we could, you know, build a raft or something, just to be on the safe side.

MARTIN   Well whatever we do, let's get out of the rain ... It's starting to bucket down.

NOAH (*from off*) I told you it would rain ...

The family narrates the passing of time.

ALL

And it just kept raining forty days,

thirty-nine nights

It just kept raining

Til the land was out of sight

So the ark took to the water

With all the beasts and birds

And the family of Noah

Who are starting to have words

Because with all this raining

Everything's soaked through

And the family of Noah

Don't know what to do.

Scene Two

Aboard Noah's Ark. The family are huddled under large black umbrellas. Noah is wearing bright yellow waterproofs. He looks like the sun.

The girls are huddled together.

SARAH   Really though, the water's looking ever so high ... Surely that's enough rain.

JUDITH   You'd think so.

MRS NOAH   It's enough rain when God says it's enough rain. Or so Noah says.

HANNAH   Well, I've had enough rain to last me a lifetime ... What I wouldn't give for a glimpse of sun.

JUDITH   The animals aren't happy.

SARAH   Of course.

JUDITH   The tiger's fur is damp, and the elephants are getting arthritis from the cold. And they keep hurting themselves when the waves are high. One of the bears bumped his head on a rafter, and now he's ... well, he's like a bear with a sore head. The giraffes have caught sore throats. The parrots are sick as parrots.

SARAH   And the camels have got the hump.

MRS NOAH   Oh dear.

HANNAH   I want to go home.

JUDITH   What home? ... It's all gone.

The boys are huddled together.

SHEM   The waters are still getting higher.

JAPETH   I wonder if anyone survived.

SHEM   I doubt it.

HAM   Everyone gone.

JAPETH   I have to say ... I'm impressed that we're floating ... I didn't really think it would ... I mean, it's so big, and none of us are boat builders by trade. So many cubits: three hundred long, fifty wide, thirty high ... I mean I'm a good enough carpenter but the biggest thing I've built up til now is a wardrobe and that's only, like, five cubits by two.

HAM   ... And that moment when the waters started rising and it was creaking and shifting and I thought – we've made a weak point or we shouldn't have put so many of the heavy animals at the bottom – and I thought – the boat's going to break in two, it's going to split right down the middle and then where will we be?

SHEM   And now look at us – bobbing along.

HAM   We're hardly bobbing ... We're dipping and diving and rocking and rolling and ... Oh no.

Ham is sick over the side.

JUDITH   Here, this tea will help with sea sickness. *(Hands Ham a mug.)*

HAM   Thanks.

HANNAH   I think I might need some too.

JUDITH   There's plenty down in the hold ... Come on everyone – let's get out of the rain. I don't want everyone catching colds. Right, Mrs Noah?

MRS NOAH   Absolutely right.

SARAH   Well, I've got a nice warming stew on the bubble ...

SHEM   What's the point of a good stew without a good bit of meat to go in it?

SARAH   I promise you – you'll hardly notice.

JAPETH   Dad? ... Dad? ... Are you coming in?

NOAH   You all go on down ... I'll be down in a minute. I like the feeling of the rain on my face.

HAM   You'd think he'd be used to it by now.

MRS NOAH   Not too long love, I don't like the sound of that cough you've got coming on – sounds like one of those walrus creatures.

They all go down ... Once they've gone:

NOAH   Errr ... 'Scuse me? ... I know you're probably very busy with all this rain and business but I wouldn't mind a quick chat ... No? ... Anyone home? ... I'll leave a message ... Listen Boss, if you are listening ... All this rain, it's extremely impressive ... but I think we might have had enough of it by now ... The world is clearly flooded. Forty days, thirty-nine nights by my count ... And what a deluge. Amazing, very mighty, very well done indeed. *(Silence)* ... It's just ... are you completely sure this was the right thing to do? ... All those people, all those souls, all that life ... Are you there? I ... I'll try again later.

He goes down.

Some of the animals sneak up to the deck. Miserable and damp. They look up to the sky and shudder. As soon as they hear noises from below they disappear again.

Japeth and Judith come up, sharing an umbrella between them.

JUDITH   Nothing like a good bowl of stew.

JAPETH   And that was nothing like a good bowl of stew.

JUDITH   Don't be mean.

JAPETH   Oh I'm not really. Sarah's a great cook ... Just ... lentils again ... it's enough to make anyone grumpy. I've never liked lentils.

From far away.

MARTIN   Help me!

JUDITH   What was that?

JAPETH   What?

MARTIN   Help me!

JUDITH   There's someone out there.

JAPETH   Quickly, go and get my brothers – and find a length of rope.

Judith goes and moments later the brothers rush up.

HAM   What's going on?

JAPETH   There's someone out there. Listen …

MARTIN   Help me!

JAPETH   It's getting closer.

Judith comes back with some rope.

JUDITH   You have to save him.

HAM   Hey … You out there … Can you paddle towards us? … We'll throw a rope down.

SHEM   We were meant to be the only survivors. That's what Dad said God said. Maybe … Maybe we're not supposed to save this man … I don't know.

HAM   Don't be an idiot, Shem.

Martin is closer.

MARTIN   Hello … Can you help me?

JAPETH   Oh … it's you … It's him … The man from home.

MARTIN   Please help me!

JUDITH   Where's your wife?

MARTIN   She fell off … She fell off the raft … Please help me … I can't hold on much longer.

HAM   Here. Grab hold of this.

SHEM   We should ask Dad.

HAM   We can't let a man drown right in front of us ... We must stand together on this ... Brothers?

JAPETH   Brothers.

HAM   Shem?

Noah comes out on deck.

NOAH   Boys? ... What's going on?

JAPETH   There's a man down here ... He's on a raft ... We're helping him up.

NOAH   Oh Lord ... Show us what to do ... Lord ... What's the right thing to do?

The women have come out too.

HANNAH   Why are you even hesitating? ... Pull him up.

HAM   I'm not strong enough ... Shem, I need your help. Shem. Please

MARTIN   I'll give you anything ... Anything you want ... Anything. Just save my life. Please.

HAM   Shem. Please.

JAPETH   I can't keep hold of the rope.

HAM   The rope's slipping.

JAPETH   Tie it to something.

HAM   Everything's too wet. Blasted rain ... Shem. Help us ... I need your help.

SHEM   Father?

NOAH   Lord?

MARTIN   Please ... Please ...

JAPETH   I'm losing him.

HAM   Grab my hand ... Grab my hand.

MRS NOAH   Careful. Don't lose Ham overboard ... Somebody hold on to Ham.

MARTIN   Just hurry up and save me.

A terrible clap of thunder and bolt of lightning. Martin is lost. A moment of silence.

NOAH   We should pray.

HAM   You pray.

JUDITH   One more life ... One more tiny life ... Are you really so angry Lord?

HAM   Why didn't you help us, Brother?

SHEM   It wasn't God's will.

HAM   A man just drowned, right in front of us – and you didn't even try to help save him. The last man alive on Earth other than us ... We've always done things as brothers.

SHEM   When they're the right things.

HAM   That was the right thing.

SHEM   Father?

NOAH   He was a sinner ... God/

MRS NOAH   Leave it for now, love ... I don't think ... I mean ... Right now ... Just ... Oh if only it would stop raining ... This endless rain.

SARAH   If only it would stop raining.

JUDITH   If only it would stop raining.

HANNAH   If only it would stop raining.

BOYS   If only it would stop raining.

NOAH   Lord ... I really do think that might be enough rain now.

And it stops raining.

NOAH   Thank you Lord ... *(Quietly)* Crystal clear, Lord.

JUDITH   One more soul, Lord ... One last tiny soul. Was it so much/

MRS NOAH   Hush Judith ... Will you look at that ? Not a cloud in the sky. Amazing ... I feel better already ... Don't we all?

NOAH   Another mighty miracle.

JAPETH   Gosh – I can see everything. The water's smooth as a piece of glass. It stretches for such a long way ... we're in the middle of nowhere ... Where are we?

HANNAH   It's so still. Thank the heavens for that ... So. What happens now? Which way are we going?

NOAH   The Lord will show us the way. You just need a little more faith ... You've just got to trust/

MRS NOAH   Come on, let's get out of these wet things ...

Time passes. Some animals come out on deck, shake the rain out of their fur and feathers and enjoy the sunshine for a while.

Sarah and Hannah are sunbathing. Shem and Ham are playing a game. Judith and Japeth are cleaning things. Noah and Mrs Noah are asleep.

The 'Noah's Ark' sign has graffiti on it now with all of their names added. It looks rather weather-beaten.

Japeth looks overboard.

JAPETH   I'm sure that whale is staring at me ... It looks hungry.

HAM   C5.

SHEM   Hit.

HAM   C6.

SHEM   Hit.

HAM   C7.

SHEM   Hit.

HAM   C8.

SHEM   You sunk my Noah's Ark.

HAM   Ha ha ... What a game ... I love it ...

SHEM   You play this way too much.

HAM   Another go?

SARAH   Oh give it a rest, Ham.

HANNAH   I've had enough of that awful game ... Every day for as long as I can remember, since we've been stuck here without a hint of a breeze, all you want to do is play that awful game.

SARAH   You know what I miss? ... I miss flowers.

HANNAH   Me too ... And I'd love a breeze. Just a gentle breeze ... I'm suffocating here.

HAM   Go on, Brother? Play me again. Will you? Please.

JAPETH   I could do with a break.

SHEM   I'd rather clean bird droppings off the deck than lose again.

NOAH   I'm not sure I approve of a game that involves so much sinking.

They start to play.

SARAH   I'll take over from you, Judith, if you like.

JUDITH   Thanks, Sarah. I wouldn't mind going down to check on the animals.

SARAH   I don't know how you can bear it ... They stink in this heat and if we let them out, they get everywhere.

A fly buzzes around Mrs Noah. Without thinking, she swats at it; the buzzing stops. She realises what she's done. Horror. Then it starts buzzing again – a relief.

HANNAH   What a beautiful sunset. The one hundred and forty ninth beautiful sunset.

SHEM   You know, the other day I fell asleep and a toad jumped right in my mouth. I felt a little hoarse for days after getting that frog in my throat.

They all groan.

SHEM   What? ... What? ... I've been working on that for days.

HANNAH   Well, the other day, I stepped in a poodle and a cat landed on my head. I thought to myself – oh no, it's raining cats and dogs.

They groan again.

MRS NOAH   Please ... Children ... No more jokes.

SARAH   It's just a way of passing the time.

HANNAH   I was wondering. Why didn't the worms come into the ark in an apple?

SARAH   I don't know.

HANNAH   Because everything came in pairs.

MRS NOAH   We have to get off this boat. Noah, do you hear me?

JAPETH   D10

HAM   Oh no. You sunk my Noah's Ark.

JAPETH   Ha ha.

They carry on.

NOAH *(quietly, to the heavens)* Errr? ... Hello? ... Are you there? It's only me again.

MRS NOAH   Is He there?

NOAH   He might be busy.

MRS NOAH   Doing what precisely? That's what I'd like to know ... There's nothing left to do. He saw to that.

NOAH   Lord? ... Just a little thing.

MRS NOAH   If He's there tell him that the stocks are running low, that Sarah's an expert with lentils but it's enough already. My stomach won't take any more. Just tell Him. No more lentils.

NOAH   I don't think we can bother the Lord Almighty with something as small as lentils.

MRS NOAH   And ask Him which way we're going if we're going anywhere at all ... Does He answer you? ... You do still hear His voice, don't you?

NOAH   I ... I'm sure He's still there ... still looking out for us ... I ... I trust him, just like before.

MRS NOAH   And I trust you my love ... But the store cupboard is nearly empty and we can't live on sunshine ... We could always ... you know ...

NOAH   No.

MRS NOAH   A nice bit of goat in the stew ... It would raise everyone's spirits.

NOAH   Woman – I said NO.

MRS NOAH   Don't you use that tone with me, you miserable old man ... I'll go and see how Judith's getting on ... You try and get an answer out of him ... Come on children ... Come down to the hold with me, it's almost dinner time and I think your father needs a little alone time with God.

They go.

The daylight has faded and the stars have come out.

NOAH *(prayer)*

Lord, the food is getting lower

And the boat can't go much slower

And I think You should know

Just what the trouble is

Lord. My kids are bored

The animals are greedy

My wife's a wreck

And I don't mean to seem needy

And I think You should know

Just what the trouble is

And I'm all alone here

On this endless sea

So small and alone here

No closer to Thee

And so my Lord, please hear my plea

I'm begging You

Is there anything that You can do?

Lord. You move in mysterious ways

But we haven't spoken for days

And I think You should know

Just what the trouble is

Lord, I don't know how to cope

And I don't want to lose hope

But I think You should know I need a sign

And I'm all alone here

On this endless sea

So small and alone here

No closer to Thee

And so my Lord, please hear my plea

I'm begging You

Is there anything that You can do?

I need a sign. I need a sign

A wind picks up. The boat tilts suddenly.

NOAH   Thank you Lord ... Thank you ... Crystal clear, Lord. Absolutely crystal clear.

Everyone rushes back.

NOAH   I told you He hadn't forgotten us.

SARAH   Everything in the galley fell off the shelves.

HANNAH   I've bruised my leg.

HAM   We're moving.

SHEM   Where are we going?

NOAH   We're heading home, children.

MRS NOAH   Home? ... I thought ...

NOAH   A new home ... Just a little more patience now ... let the wind take us where we're meant to go ... Doesn't it feel wonderful? Having the wind on our faces, drying out our clothes, shaking all through our bones ... I feel alive ... Don't you all? ... How marvellous ... And to think ... a moment ago I felt so wretched.

HAM   Oh no. The wind's making the boat rock ... and roll ... and tilt ... not the tilting.

He rushes to the side, but before he can be sick ...

HAM   Hey, look at this – I think the water's going down.

HANNAH   Really? How can you tell?

HAM   I think I can see some rocks below the water. I couldn't see them before.

HANNAH   Oh yes, you're right.

JUDITH   Drop a line over the side then we'll know if it's really going down.

SARAH   Is it true? Is the water going down?

HAM   Thank goodness. We can be off this god-forsaken boat.

NOAH   I don't like that language, my boy.

HAM   But/

NOAH   God has not forsaken this boat ... The Lord continues to look after us, and guide us. We should pray.

HAM   Pray to the God who drowned every other soul on the planet? ... A fine God to do a thing like that.

NOAH   How dare you? How dare you blaspheme like that?

HANNAH   Shh Ham ... Leave it.

JAPETH   Brother – this is not the time.

HAM   I don't know how you can pray to a God that would do such a terrible thing ... Kill everyone, everyone we know – all our friends, and everyone else. And all the animals – other than the lucky few ... And then just stick us on a boat and forget about us for so long that we're almost crazy with boredom. We're all thinking it, just no-one's brave enough to say it. It's blowing a gale now.

NOAH   Such ingratitude. Such wickedness. I should have left you to drown.

HAM   I wish you had ... What's waiting for us now? What's out there waiting for us now?

NOAH   I pleaded with Him. I argued with Him for you. For all of you. He didn't want to save you. I made Him. It was the bravest thing I ever did, bargaining with God. 'God,' I said, 'I'll build you your boat, I'll save your animals, but my family come too. I'm not going anywhere without them .' And now you throw it back in my face ... What an idiot I am.

HAM   How could you be part of such a plan?

NOAH   I do what my God tells me to do.

HAM   You are weak ... You're a weak old man.

SHEM   How dare you? ... How dare you speak to our father like that?

Shem launches at Ham – Japeth keeps them apart.

JAPETH   Father? Ham doesn't mean it ... Look at what you've done.

NOAH *(to Ham)* I curse you ... I curse you, your wife and all your children ... I never want to see you again.

JAPETH   It's just the wind, Father ... After so many days of being so still ... It's made us jumpy. And Ham's never been good at being cooped up. That's all. He loves you. We all love you.

SHEM   Ham's just young, Father. He doesn't know what he's saying.

HAM   I ... I'm sorry, Father ... Dad? ... I'm sorry ... Please ... It was the wind – it pulled the words out of me. I ... I didn't mean to upset you. Dad ... I love you ... Don't ... don't look at me like that.

But Noah turns from him.

MRS NOAH   The sooner we're off the water, the better.

JAPETH   My legs are itching for a really good run.

JUDITH   Or a dance ... If only we could dance ... Well, why don't we?

MRS NOAH   In this wind?

JUDITH   What better time? ... There's nothing else to do ... The animals are safe ... Come on husband. Dance with me. Come on girls. Let's dance. We won't fall overboard. God will keep us safe ... Come on. Let's dance while the waters go down.

They dance with each other and the wind ... Every so often one of them checks the water level and gives the thumbs up to the others.

Suddenly the boat screeches to a halt.

Hannah screams.

HANNAH   We've hit something … The boat's hit something …
We're going to drown. We're going to drown.

JUDITH   I'll check on the animals.

JAPETH   I'll check the hull. Shem. With me.

Japeth, Judith and Shem go.

HAM   The water's definitely down from where it was.

SARAH   Are we still moving?

HANNAH   I can't tell.

SARAH   Maybe we've reached our destination.

HANNAH   Maybe we're all going to die.

NOAH   You're not going to … Will you ever …? Oh what's
the point?

Japeth and Shem return.

JAPETH   The boat's stuck on a rock.

SHEM   There's no water coming in.

Judith returns.

JAPETH   I think that we're on the top of a mountain.

MRS NOAH   We're what now?

NOAH   Of course – a mountain … The waters must have
gone down enough – we can't see the rest of it yet but there's a
mountain down there – and we're at the very top. Not long and
we'll be able to get off.

HANNAH   How will we know when?

NOAH   There'll be a sign.

JAPETH   Father? Why don't we send a bird in a few day's time. What do you think? Don't you think that could work?

JUDITH   What kind of bird?

JAPETH   A raven ... Easy to see the black feathers against the sky and they're good straight fliers ... We'll send him out and ... if he doesn't come back we'll know he's found land.

NOAH   Ravens are clever birds ... Japeth, my son, it's a good idea. Now, Judith come down to the animals with me. I want to check on them.

Judith and Noah go into the hold.

HAM   Just got to wait ... Always wait ... More of this infernal waiting ... I can't bear it ... I ... I shouldn't have said those things. Should I? He looked so/

SHEM   Come on. I'll play your game with you ... It'll help to pass the time ... Don't feel too badly, Brother.

HAM   I just ... I didn't ... I didn't want to upset him. I just ... I just feel so/

Shem and Ham reconcile.

MRS NOAH   Well, I might just go and cook up a nice dinner of something. Maybe there's something special stuck at the back of the store cupboard.

Time passes. The animals creep onto the deck to have a look over the side then scurry back to their hiding places.

Judith comes back to the deck with a raven.

JAPETH   It's time. Look, there's a good few feet of rock below the ark now.

NOAH   Yes. Judith, give me the bird.

JUDITH   I've been feeding him up specially – he's a strong one ... and clever.

NOAH   Go on then my friend ... Fly high and find land for us ... Let us know if there is anything above water other than this mountain top.

He throws the raven into the air. It flies up and up.

SARAH   There he goes.

Everyone watches him.

SHEM   Just a speck now.

JAPETH   I can't see him any more. Did he fall into the sea?

NOAH   Just flown out of view, that's all.

HAM   Father ... I/

SARAH   I think I see him again. Yes ... yes, he's coming back.

The raven returns.

JUDITH   He's not flying straight. He's hurt. No, he's just exhausted.

The raven falls onto the deck.

JUDITH   Poor bird. Poor bird.

HANNAH   No land yet then. We're still stuck at the top of the mountain. This is even worse than being lost at sea.

NOAH   We were never lost. We were just making our way here.

A moment.

NOAH   We'll try again in a few days.

JUDITH   You'll have to send another bird. The raven won't be strong enough.

Time passes. The animals creep onto the deck to have another look over the side. They are more excited now.

NOAH   Right. Gather round all. I think it's time to try again … Sarah go and fetch one of the doves. Go and fetch Etta. She'll be the one to find land for us.

MRS NOAH   Are you sure. Little Etta? What if she doesn't come back.

NOAH   She'll come back. Don't worry, my love.

SARAH   Here she is. Her little heart is beating so fast.

NOAH   Go on then my Etta. Fly and find us land.

He releases the dove.

HANNAH   I can't see her.

SARAH   She's disappeared.

JAPETH   She's too pale and the sky's too light.

JUDITH   We'll never know now.

MRS NOAH   If there's land she'll come back and tell us. She'll find a way. That dove – you know, when we were at home she'd come into the kitchen and sit and coo at me while I worked. We've had her since she was an egg. She's not just one of these creatures who turned up to take a place on the ark. She's one of the family.

They wait. The animals poke their heads out of their hiding places.

HANNAH   Can anyone see her?

They wait some more. The animals crane their necks a bit further out.

JUDITH   She won't be able to keep flying much longer.

NOAH   She'll be back.

HAM   Father … I/

NOAH   Look – here she comes.

The dove returns with something in her beak.

MRS NOAH   Etta. Etta my little dove. You've come back to us. What's this?

SHEM   She's carrying a twig.

JAPETH   It's from an olive tree.

HAM   An olive branch.

NOAH   There's trees. The water's down as far as the tops of the trees. Oh well done, little one.

ETTA   Very well done. Not long now my family. Another week or so is all. That's all. Then we can get off the ark and start building our lives again.

HAM   Father, I'm sorry.

NOAH   I know you are, son. I know you are.

HAM   Can you forgive me?

NOAH   I can try.

They have a moment.

Time passes. The animals no longer contain their excitement.

SHEM   Right, come on. It's been another week. Let's do it ... Come on.

JAPETH   Don't rush him.

NOAH   I'm coming. I'm coming. Ready, my Etta. Now, this time, don't come back. If there's land, don't come back. I'll know then. I'll know it's time to leave ... And I'll send your husband after you. Are you ready? ... Fly safe and once we're settled feel free to come and visit. Lord ... take good care of my little Etta. Here she goes.

He releases the dove. She flies away.

JAPETH   I think it's been long enough. She hasn't come back ... She's found land. Father?

NOAH   Yes, my son. I believe you are right. I believe you are right indeed.

MRS NOAH *(whispers to Noah)* Perhaps we should be completely sure.

NOAH   A good idea my love. Let's release all the birds. Let's see them all flying up into the air, finding their new homes. Judith? Japeth? Will you do the honours?

They open the hatch. All the birds fly up into the air singing madly. They fly around their heads then up and away. It is a completely beautiful moment and they are all awestruck.

NOAH   Pack up everything girls. We're heading off. Boys – with me, let's release the animals.

The animals are, noisily, delighted.

NOAH   Hold on. Hold on. There's an order. An order. Small fast things first. Then slow small things. Then slow large things. And last of all the big fast dangerous beasts. Let's give the little ones a chance to get away before the vegetarian pledge runs out.

The boys go, the girls lean over and watch.

MRS NOAH Look, look, they're opening the big door! Here they come.

JUDITH   Look! There go the rabbits, the hares, the cats and dogs, the rats and the mice. Look how fast they run. *(Silence)* I feel like I'm losing my friends.

MRS NOAH You've done a good job of keeping them all alive, Judith dear.

SARAH   Oh look! Here come the frogs, the lizards, the baboons ... all heading off in different directions.

HANNAH   Now here come the big beasts. The elephants, the giraffes, the wildebeest, the woolly mammoth.

SARAH   And here come the others ... look how fast the lion's running, and the cheetahs, and tigers, all the big cats – and those awful crocodiles.

JUDITH   Gosh, so many creatures ... I got so used to them, I forgot how many there were. What a parade ... Not long and the earth will be full of animals again.

Noah returns.

NOAH   We're all done ... I've sent the boys down ... They're waiting for you on the beach.

HANNAH   The beach?

NOAH   Of course. We're still by the water, after all ... it'll take a bit longer before it goes completely. Go on, go down and join them.

MRS NOAH   Noah?

NOAH   I'll just ... give me a moment ... just to say goodbye.

The women go.

NOAH   ... Are You there? ... Thank you ... We're very nearly home and dry ... Very nearly ... I know You're up there ... I know it ... I had a moment. Just a moment when I wasn't sure. And I've never felt so lonely. But now I know. Stay close ... I still need You ... I don't know what's waiting for me ... This was my adventure ... And what do I do now? I'm just a simple man ... All I wanted was to serve You and to keep my family safe. (*Sees the 'Noah's Ark' sign.*) Well, I know I'm always badgering You for signs. Maybe I should just take my own one for now.

He leaves the ark.

Scene Three

On the shore of a brand new beach. They all stand around happy in the sunshine, a few suitcases scattered about.

NOAH   Here we are children, standing on the shore of a whole new world. Feel that sand between your toes. You're the first to feel it. This sand my children, this sand will always be your sand. This water will never be so crystal clear again. When you were born, I held you in my arms and I wanted to give you the world – and I have. It's a big responsibility. The biggest. Don't mess it up. Whatever you do – don't mess it up.

MRS NOAH   Well said, my love.

SHEM   Oh the sand. Sarah did you ever feel such sand?

JAPETH   Look at the trees – beautiful wood – I will build tables and chairs for everyone.

HAM   I rather fancy a swim.

HANNAH   You are perverse! I'd have thought you'd be sick of the sight of water.

HAM   And after I've been for a swim I shall climb a tree and roll all over in the sand and then I'll go for a swim again and then a run and then I shall catch a turkey and roast it on a fire on the beach.

SHEM   It sounds like a very good plan, Brother.

HAM   And I will lie on my back and feel the stars gazing down on me and not the infernal rocking of that boat.

JAPETH   We will find a forest, Judith. And I will make beautiful things. And we will have a whole family of carpenters. And they will all be good good children.

JUDITH   Of course.

SARAH   What of us Shem? Where will we go?

SHEM   Wherever you like, my Sarah. Somewhere warm I think. Somewhere, we can rest.

NOAH   So, go on children. Go and find new homes. Come to visit us on occasion. Bring the grandchildren round.

MRS NOAH   ... Lots and lots of grandchildren.

SHEM   And the Lord will be with us?

SARAH   What if He just does it all again? Washes us all away? If He's done it once/

NOAH *(shouts)* Lord? ... Lord? ... They need a sign. One last sign and then I'll leave You alone for the rest of my days. Something ... Something to show them that You'll never do this again. Please. If You wouldn't mind.

A rainbow appears. Magnificent. Glorious. Breathtaking.

NOAH   Crystal clear, Lord. Thank you.

The dove flies down and lands on Noah's shoulder.

The animals creep forwards and form a protective circle around the family.

Lights down.

The end.

Aurora Metro Books

some of our other play collections

PLAYS FOR YOUTH THEATRES AND LARGE CASTS by Neil Duffield

ISBN 978-1-906582-06-7 £12.99

THEATRE CENTRE: Plays for Young People introduced by Rosamunde Hutt

ISBN 978-0-954233-05-1 £12.99

BLACK AND ASIAN PLAYS ANTHOLOGY introduced by Afia Nkrumah

ISBN 978-0-953675-74-6 £12.99

YOUNG BLOOD plays for young performers ed. Sally Goldsworthy

ISBN 978-0-9515877-6-8 £12.99

PLAYS FOR YOUNG PEOPLE by Charles Way

ISBN 978-0-953675-71-5 £9.95

THE CLASSIC FAIRYTALES Retold for the Stage by Charles Way

ISBN 978-0-954233-00-6 £11.50

THE CLASSIC FAIRY TALES 2 Retold for the Stage by Charles Way

ISBN 978-0-955156-67-0 £11.99

NEW PLAYS FOR YOUNG PEOPLE by Charles Way

ISBN 978-1-906582-51-7 £12.99

NEW SOUTH AFRICAN PLAYS ed. Charles J. Fourie

ISBN 978-0-954233-01-3 £11.99

BALKAN PLOTS: New Plays from Central and Eastern Europe ed. Cheryl Robson

ISBN 978-0-953675-73-9 £9.95

www.aurorametro.com